Souled Out

ALLOWING CHRIST TO LIVE THROUGH YOU

BILL HUGHES

LifeWay Press®
Nashville, Tennessee

ISBN: 0633193925

This book is a resource in the "Bible Studies" category of the
Christian Growth Study Plan. Course CG-1021

Dewey Decimal Classification Number: 248.83
Subject Heading: CHRISTIAN LIFE \ YOUTH—RELIGIOUS LIFE

Unless otherwise noted, all Scripture quotations are taken from the
Holman Christian Standard Bible®
Copyright © 1999, 2000, 2002, 2003 by Holman Bible Publishers.
Used by permission.

The photography in this book is not intended to represent the actual persons
that are described in text and is for illustrative purposes only.

Printed in the United States of America.

Student Ministry Publishing
LifeWay Christian Resources
of the Southern Baptist Convention
One LifeWay Plaza
Nashville, TN 37234-0174

CONTENTS

ABOUT THE AUTHOR

Bill Hughes became a Christian in 1971 at the Citadel in Charleston, South Carolina. He graduated from the University of Central Florida, where he played soccer, and the Southern Baptist Theological Seminary in Louisville, Kentucky, where he nearly froze to death.

He has been a youth minister for 31 years. For 11 years he was Minister of Youth at Second Baptist in College Park, Georgia; and for the last 15 he has been Minister of Youth, College, and Singles at First Baptist Church in Tifton, Georgia.

Bill has led youth on mission trips to 10 countries as well as 13 states. At least 43 of his former youth are serving as ministers. Seven are international missionaries.

When asked why so many former youth have gone into the ministry he replies, "I have no idea, but maybe after being around me they saw that God could do something with just ordinary people."

His wife, Dana, has been leading mission teams to mainland China for the past decade. They have two children, Elizabeth and Christina.

Bill runs an average of five miles per day. He also loves to watch and play sports, especially baseball, basketball, football, and golf. He is a huge fan of the University of Alabama.

He is the author of *Living Pure Inside Out*, which was published by LifeWay in 2002.

HOW TO USE THIS BOOK

This study is designed to be interactive. That means that you don't just read the material; you interact with the material. Some questions require you to write a short answer. Some questions are multiple choice. And some questions require you to fill in the blanks.

For the fill-in-the-blank questions, the first letter of the correct word is given. To find the correct answer for the fill-in-the-blank activities, you will need to look in the *Holman Christian Standard Bible®* (HCSB®). All Scripture quotations are taken from this translation. If you don't have a copy of the *Holman Christian Standard Bible®* you can find it online at *www.lifeway.com.*

At the end of each session you will find discussion questions under the heading "Talk About...." These questions are for group discussion; however, if you are studying this on your own, you might want to write down each question and a short answer in your journal. Individuals or groups can also use these questions for reviewing the previous session at the beginning of each new session.

Your leader has the option of conducting this study for either 6 weeks or 15 weeks.

Six-Session Approach
If you will be studying this book for six weeks, you will have personal Bible study during the week. Each of the six chapters is divided into five sections. We recommend that you study one section a day.

Fifteen-Session Approach
If you will be studying this book for 15 weeks, you will complete these chapters during your sessions. Seven days of quiet time guides are given at the beginning of each chapter for you to study.

CHAPTER 1

THE NATURE OF PEACE

We begin our study of *Souled Out* by looking at our minds. When we are souled out, the Holy Spirit is in control of our minds; and He brings us peace. Peace of mind is God's desire for every Christian, yet so few believers are experiencing true peace.

The Big Picture

This week you will discover the following:
- ☐ How your soul relates to your spirit and body.
- ☐ Why the mind is the foundation of the soul.
- ☐ The true nature of peace.
- ☐ Where peace comes from.
- ☐ How to allow your mind to be controlled by the Holy Spirit.

As you read and study each day, begin with prayer. Ask God to speak to you, revealing the truth to you. God knows more about you, your soul, and your mind than you know. He desires to teach you so that you can live by faith, turning every aspect of your life over to Him.

Scripture

This week memorize and meditate on 2 Thessalonians 3:16.

For your private devotional reading this week, read the first three chapters in Ephesians.
Day 1—Ephesians 1:1-10
Day 2—Ephesians 1:11-14
Day 3—Ephesians 1:15-23
Day 4—Ephesians 2:1-10
Day 5—Ephesians 2:11-22
Day 6—Ephesians 3:1-13
Day 7—Ephesians 3:14-21

Prayer Thought

I often have a "prayer thought" I carry with me during the day to keep me focused on God and what He is doing. I will say this prayer to Him several times a day. This week, make this your prayer thought: *Father, control my mind and bring me Your peace. Your peace, Lord, Your peace.*

MEMORY VERSE

May the Lord of peace Himself give you peace always in every way. The Lord be with all of you (2 Thess. 3:16).

✦ DAY 1: BODY, SOUL, AND SPIRIT

Katie is a Christian. She knows that for sure! But she has such horrible thoughts. She often wonders how anyone who is a Christian could think such terrible things. She feels like there is a war going on inside her. One side wants to do the right thing, and the other side is just out of control. The harder she tries to wipe bad thoughts from her mind, the more frustrated she becomes. She fears she will eventually act on her thoughts, and that scares her even more than the thoughts themselves.

When she finally talked to a school counselor about her problem, the counselor told her not to worry. She explained that everyone experiences those types of thoughts. Katie didn't buy that, but she sure didn't know what was going on.

What do you think Katie's problem is?_____
_____
_____
_____

1-A NEW YOU

Have you ever turned from your sins and placed your faith in Jesus Christ? If you have, the Bible says something pretty spectacular has taken place.

> If anyone is in Christ, there is a new creation; old things have passed away, and look, new things have come (2 Cor. 5:17).

Read 2 Corinthians 5:17. What does this verse say happened to you? Check all that apply.
- ☐ **Old things have passed away.**
- ☐ **Old things are now new things.**
- ☐ **New things have come.**
- ☐ **You are a new creation.**

> I no longer live, but Christ lives in me (Gal. 2:20).

When you came to Christ, you became a new creation. As a new creation, Jesus Christ now lives in you. In fact, according to Galatians 2:20:

"I no longer l_____, but C_____ l_____ in m_____."

Souled Out

What is the difference between the old you and the new you? Read Romans 8:9. How does this verse describe the difference between the old you and the new you?_____

_____

_____

> You, however, are not in the flesh, but in the spirit, since the Spirit of God lives in you (Rom. 8:9).

2-YOUR BODY

You are a brand-new person! That is fantastic. But there is one problem—you still live in the same old physical body. Your physical body, sometimes called "the flesh" or "the sinful nature" in the Bible, did not change when you came to Christ.

The problem is not that our bodies are impure. We shouldn't hate the human body; it is a part of God's creation. But we must remember that the body is weak.

Read Mark 14:38. What did Jesus say about Peter's condition? Check all that apply.
- ☐ His spirit was willing.
- ☐ He needed to rest.
- ☐ He needed to eat.
- ☐ His flesh was weak.

> "Stay awake and pray, so that you won't enter into temptation. The spirit is willing, but the flesh is weak" (Mark 14:38).

In your spirit, you have power because Jesus lives there. But in your body, you are still weak. Read how Paul put it in 2 Corinthians 4:7.

If your body were strong, then you wouldn't need Christ living inside of you to control your thoughts, feelings, and actions. You could control these things yourself. But your body (your flesh) is weak because your flesh is corrupted and tainted by the sin you inherited from Adam.

> Now we have this treasure in clay jars, so that this extraordinary power may be from God and not from us (2 Cor. 4:7).

3-YOUR SOUL

In your spirit lives the Spirit of God. In fact, from a spiritual point of view, you are no longer alive. As Colossians 1:27 says …

You have "C_____ in y_____."

> God wanted to make known to those among the Gentiles the glorious wealth of this mystery, which is Christ in you, the hope of glory (Col.1:27).

Now the works of the flesh are obvious: sexual immorality, moral impurity, promiscuity, idolatry, sorcery, hatreds, strife, jealousy, outbursts of anger, selfish ambitions, dissensions, factions, envy, drunkenness, carousing, and anything similar, about which I tell you in advance (Gal. 5:19-21).

The fruit of the Spirit is love, joy, peace, patience, kindness, goodness, faith, gentleness, self-control (Gal. 5:22-23).

But your body is still alive and still weak and still prone to sin. And your flesh, or sinful nature, really wants to control your life and produce what Galatians 5:19 calls …

the "w_____ of the f_____."

Your soul then is actually the battleground of a great fight between the Spirit and your sinful nature. Your soul, sometimes thought of as your mind, emotions, and will, can actually go either way.

When Christ in the person of the Holy Spirit controls your soul, then He brings into your soul the fruit of the Spirit found in Galatians 5:22-23. Underline the character traits named in this passage.

Look at diagrams 1 and 2. Diagram 1 shows the person whose soul is controlled by the sinful nature (flesh), and diagram 2 shows the soul controlled by the Spirit.

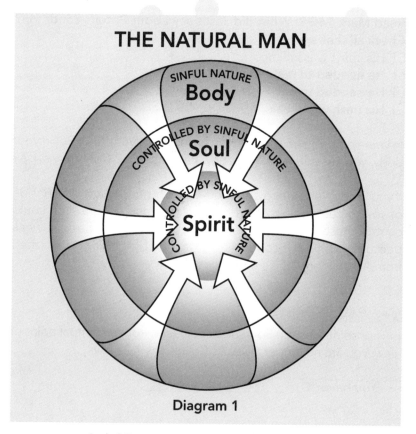

THE NATURAL MAN

SINFUL NATURE
Body

CONTROLLED BY SINFUL NATURE
Soul

CONTROLLED BY SINFUL NATURE
Spirit

Diagram 1

So Katie's real problem was probably that her mind was being controlled by her sinful nature. However, there is a better way!

4-TALK ABOUT PEACE

1. When Jesus came into your life, what actually happened?
2. Why did God leave you in a body of flesh?
3. In what ways does your sinful nature presently try to control your soul?
4. When you see the fruit of the Spirit evident in your life, how do you react?

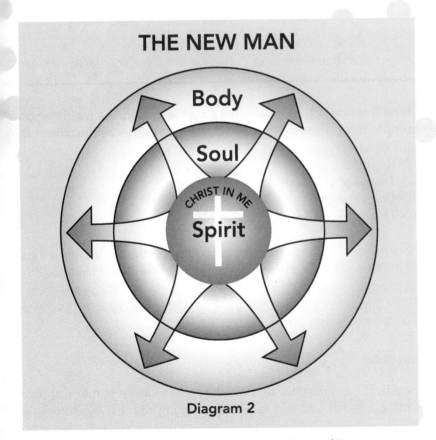

THE NEW MAN

Body

Soul

CHRIST IN ME

Spirit

Diagram 2

✦ DAY 2: THE MIND COMES FIRST

John and I have been playing golf together for 25 years. Over the years I have known about the struggles in John's life: a child with a life-threatening illness, a job that consumed his life, a paycheck that seemed too small. He experienced all the normal things that can make being an adult difficult.

Yet during all that time, John always displayed the fruit of the Spirit in his life. What made the difference? I have heard him say that he has total peace of mind knowing that he is complete in Christ. For John, peace of mind was where God's Spirit started to work.

1-AS YOU THINK

Why is what you think so important in determining everything else about your life?

Read Romans 8:5. In this verse Paul described the main things people think about. What are those two things as described in this verse?
- ☐ **Happy things**
- ☐ **Things of the flesh**
- ☐ **Deep things**
- ☐ **Things of the Spirit**

Your mind is either going to focus on things of the Spirit or on things of the flesh. And as you think, so you will become. Read Proverbs 23:7.

What this verse means is that your mind shapes who you are and who you are becoming.

2-RANDOM THOUGHTS

So what's up with those random thoughts that sometimes just pop into your head? One minute you are thinking about telling someone

Those whose lives are according to the flesh think about the things of the flesh, but those whose lives are according to the Spirit, about the things of the Spirit (Rom. 8:5).

For as he thinks within himself, so he is (Prov. 23:7).

about Jesus and then—boom!—you start thinking about the big game coming up next week.

Random thoughts are just that—random! There are two things, though, that can shape and influence your thoughts: God's Spirit living in you or your sinful nature.

James understood how the sinful nature worked. What does James 1:14 say about how we are tempted and enticed?

_____

_____

_____

_____

_____

> Each person is tempted when he is drawn away and enticed by his own evil desires (Jas. 1:14).

Sin begins in the mind. First we think it, and then we do it. But we aren't tempted by random thoughts that just appear in our minds. No, they come from our sinful natures.

Fortunately, as a Christian, you are not left to the mercy of your sin nature. God's Spirit is right there!

Read John 16:13. What did Jesus tell us about the work of God's Spirit in your life and even in your mind? _____

_____

_____

_____

_____

_____

> "When the Spirit of truth comes, He will guide you into all the truth. For He will not speak on His own, but He will speak whatever He hears. He will also declare to you what is to come" (John 16:13).

3–WHY GOD DOESN'T CONTROL OUR MINDS

Our minds generally affect our wills and emotions. The mind is open to all sorts of problems, as it can be easy prey for the flesh/sinful nature. Then why does God not control our minds since they get so messed up? After all, if our minds were permanently under His control, then we'd be home free. It all has to do with belief.

"What can we do to perform the works of God?" they asked. Jesus replied, "This is the work of God: that you believe in the One He has sent" (John 6:28-29).

The apostles said to the Lord, "Increase our faith" (Luke 17:5).

Read John 6:28-29. What does God want us to do?
☐ Attend the church of our choice
☐ Walk the straight and narrow
☐ Believe in the One He has sent
☐ Nothing

There is one primary thing God wants from us—belief. The reason God wants us to believe is because that is the only way we can have a true relationship with Him. That is why the disciples requested of Jesus in Luke 17:5 …

"I_____ our f_____."

They were realizing that faith was the only way to a relationship with God. Faith starts in the mind.

4-TALK ABOUT PEACE

1. In your life, how does what you think determine what you do?
2. What are some of the "random thoughts" you have? Where do they really come from?
3. In your mind, do you believe that Jesus is the Son of God? If so, how does that influence your relationship with God?
4. What is God teaching you about your need for peace of mind?

✸ DAY 3: WHAT IS PEACE?

In the mid-sixties through the early seventies, our country was involved in a war in the tiny Asian country of Vietnam. The Vietnam War became the first war that was broadcast live into the living rooms of America. Every night on the evening news, America viewed horrible images of its young men being critically wounded or killed. Eventually many people, especially young people, became so enraged at the human suffering they saw that they started what was known as the "Peace Movement."

The Peace Movement was sometimes organized, sometimes spontaneous, often destructive, and generally demoralizing for the soldiers watching their friends die in Vietnam. As a college student during those turbulent days, I can remember asking some of my fellow students who were "working for peace" the simple question: "Just what is peace?"

Surprisingly, the people protesting for peace were not at peace with themselves nor were they very peaceable with those around them. For them, peace was a cause. But it was a cause they often did not understand.

1—BIBLICAL PEACE

Everybody, except for a few confused individuals, wants peace. But when you talk to different people, you will get diverse ideas about peace. Some people think peace is simply the absence of conflict, while others think peace is a personal thing that emanates from the center of one's being.

What about you? How would you describe or define peace? Write your own definition of peace. _____
_____
_____
_____
_____
_____

The best way to understand peace is from a biblical point of view. The Bible mentions peace at least 449 times. When the heavenly host announced Jesus' birth in Luke 2:14, peace was the one thing the angels declared to men. Paul often began his letters by sending greetings of peace to his audience. Jesus Himself even greeted His followers after His resurrection.

What did He say in John 20:19? _____
_____

In the Old Testament, the word for *peace* is *shalom*, which means "completeness, soundness, and good welfare." Interestingly, *shalom* comes from a more primitive Hebrew word, *shalam*. (Primitive means it was older.) *Shalam* means "to pay."[1] When the Hebrews thought of peace (shalom) they thought of completeness, soundness, and good welfare; and that took place because somebody had to pay.

> In the evening of that first day of the week, the disciples were gathered together with the doors locked because of their fear of the Jews. Then Jesus came, stood among them, and said to them, "Peace to you!" (John 20:19).

In the New Testament, the Greek word for *peace* is *eirene* (pronounced i-ray-nay). *Eirene* at its heart means "harmonious relationships." *Eirene* came from the verb *eiro*, which means "to join."[2] The basic concept of peace in the New Testament is that two things are in harmony when they are joined together. In a sense, the two are united, have become one, and are at peace with each other.

Peace in the Bible is both something outward (unity/harmony) and inward (completeness/soundness). This was Paul's prayer for the church at Thessalonica.

> **May the Lord of peace Himself give you peace always in every way. The Lord be with all of you (2 Thess. 3:16).**

Read 2 Thessalonians 3:16. Paul prayed for God to give the church peace ...

"A_____ in e_____ w_____."

What do you think it means to have peace at all times and in every way? _____
_____
_____
_____

2–THE PRICE OF PEACE

Peace is available for all people. In Matthew 11:28, Jesus invited people to come to Him for rest.

> **"Come to Me, all you who are weary and burdened, and I will give you rest" (Matt. 11:28).**

Who does Jesus invite to find rest and peace?
- ☐ His followers
- ☐ Everybody who is weary
- ☐ Keepers of the law
- ☐ Christians

Peace is for all, but it is not free. Remember that *shalom* (peace) came from the word that means "to pay." Peace had to be bought because the people were neither complete nor unified in any way. In the relationship between the people and God, there was no unity.

> **Because all the fullness was pleased to dwell in Him, and to reconcile everything to Himself through Him by making peace through the blood of His cross—whether things on earth or things in heaven (Col. 1:19-20).**

According to Colossians 1:19-20, what was the price of peace?
_____
_____

The price of peace between God and man and the price of peace in our hearts was the death of Jesus.

3-WHERE DOES PEACE COME FROM?

Since you are a Christian, you would assume the answer to that question would be J_____.

If you wrote "Jesus," you are right. Read John 14:27. What does this verse tell us about peace?

☐ It belongs to Jesus.
☐ It comes from Jesus.
☐ It is a free gift.
☐ It is a fearful thing.

"Peace I leave with you. My peace I give to you. I do not give to you as the world gives. Your heart must not be troubled or fearful" (John 14:27).

Peace, as completeness and unity, actually belongs to Jesus. It is His to give away or hold onto as He wishes.

Read Ephesians 2:14a. What does this verse say about peace?

_____
_____
_____
_____

He [Jesus] is our peace (Eph. 2:14).

4-TALK ABOUT PEACE

1. Do you ever wonder what peace really is?
2. Why do you think the Bible is the best place to learn about peace?
3. Which is easier for you to understand, inner peace or outer peace?
4. What does the fact that Jesus paid the price for peace mean to you?

✸ DAY 4: A HUNT FOR PEACE

David is an interesting character in the Old Testament. He began his political/military career by killing the giant Goliath. Ultimately, he became a great military leader and led many successful campaigns that resulted in a great expansion of Israel's territory.

Even though David was such a great warrior, he often wrote of peace. Why was David so concerned with peace?

Read Psalm 37:37. David said,

> "The man of peace will have a f_____."

David, the warrior that he was, knew something that most people never pick up on. Real peace is from God, and the only way to have a meaningful future is with God as well. So the man who has peace from God also has a future from God.

3-PRINCE OF PEACE

Some people believe that Jesus is the road to peace. Since they believe this they often try to resolve conflicts by asking Jesus to help them find peace in a situation. Jesus doesn't lead us to peace; Jesus is peace.

You're probably asking, "How can Jesus be peace?" From Day 3 we learned that peace is outward unity/harmony and inward completeness/soundness. Only Jesus is both of these!

JESUS IS COMPLETE—INWARDLY
By His very nature, Jesus is complete. He is completely God.

In Him [Christ] the entire fullness of God's nature dwells bodily (Col. 2:9).

Read Colossians 2:9. What does it say about the deity of Christ?
- ☐ Christ is a part of God.
- ☐ Christ reflects God.
- ☐ Christ is sent from God.
- ☐ Christ is God.

JESUS IS UNIFIED—OUTWARDLY
Yes, Jesus Christ is completely and totally God. Moreover, there is total unity and harmony between the Father and the Son.

"May they all be one, just as You, Father, are in Me and I am in You. May they also be one in Us, so that the world may believe You sent Me" (John 17:21).

Read Jesus' prayer for us in John 17:21. How did Jesus describe the relationship between Himself and the Father? _____
_____
_____
_____

Souled Out

Since perfect unity and harmony exist in the relationship between the Father, the Son, and the Spirit, peace flows from their relationship. In fact, the relationship between Father, Son, and Spirit is the true source of all peace. Isaiah understood this.

Isaiah declared in Isaiah 9:6-7 that Jesus would be known as ...

"W_____ C_____, M_____
G_____, E_____ F_____ and
P_____ of P_____."

Isaiah described the coming Messiah in many ways that we understand God. The result is found in Isaiah 9:7. In other words, the unity (peace) between the Father, Son, and Spirit will continue to increase forever.

2-PURSUING PEACE

Since peace comes from Jesus and since Jesus Himself is peace, the question arises, "How do we pursue peace?" Or, should we even try to pursue peace?

In some ways we really can't go on a hunt to find peace. After all, how can we possibly, on our own, find or create completeness in our spirits? How can we, on our own, possibly create unity between us and other people? How can we, in our own strength, achieve unity between us and God?

The answer is found in Psalm 34:14. What did David say?

"S_____ p_____ and p_____ it."

So what is up? Are we to pursue peace, to seek it, even though we know that in our own strength and power we can never find it? The answer lies in knowing what it means to pursue and knowing where to pursue.

The word *pursue* in Hebrew means to "follow after" something. It is generally used to describe "following after" an enemy you hope to overtake and destroy.[3] But peace is no enemy. When we pursue peace, we are following after peace.

For a child will be born for us, a son will be given to us, and the government will be on His shoulders. He will be named Wonderful Counselor, Mighty God, Eternal Father, Prince of Peace (Isa. 9:6).

The dominion will be vast, and its prosperity will never end (Isa. 9:7).

Turn away from evil and do good; seek peace and pursue it (Ps. 34:14).

But where? Where is the peace that we are to follow after? People look for peace in many places.

Check below the places you have seen people look for peace (completeness and unity).

☐ **In the family**
☐ **In a relationship**
☐ **In church**
☐ **In a cause**
☐ **In nature**

3-THE END OF THE HUNT

People look for peace in all those places listed above. But the pursuit of real peace takes us to the Holy Spirit, who is within us.

The fruit of the Spirit is love, joy, peace, patience, kindness, goodness, faith, gentleness, self-control (Gal. 5:22-23).

Read Galatians 5:22-23. List the traits the Holy Spirit gives.

_____
_____
_____
_____
_____
_____

This verse describes the fruit of the Spirit. The fruit of the Spirit is what the Spirit produces in our souls when we are out of the way, or souled out.

To find peace, to pursue peace, to hunt peace down and take it captive, we turn to God. Our spirit abides with God's Spirit, the source of peace.

4-TALK ABOUT PEACE

1. Why is Jesus the true source of peace?
2. Where, if anywhere, have you looked in your search for peace?
3. Why do you think the Bible tells us to pursue peace when we know we can't just make peace happen?
4. In your life, do you see completeness and unity? If yes, describe what it is like.

DAY 5: THE SPIRIT-CONTROLLED MIND

1–PURSUING PEACE OF MIND

As we have seen, peace is outward unity as well as inward completeness. When we pursue peace of mind, we are pursuing inward completeness, or soundness, of mind.

So how do we do that? Pursuing inner peace is allowing our minds to be controlled by the Spirit and seeing, understanding, and believing that we are already complete in Christ.

FIRST—CONTROLLED BY THE SPIRIT

As long as you control your own mind, you will never have inner peace. But there is good news! Your mind already belongs to God. Read 1 Corinthians 2:6-16 in your Bible. This passage can be summarized as follows: It is impossible for the human mind to do or know anything spiritual; but Christians have the Holy Spirit inside of them, and therefore, have the mind of Christ.

What does this passage mean to you? _____
_____
_____
_____
_____
_____

When your mind is under the Holy Spirit's control, He will then teach you about your completeness in Christ.

SECOND—WE SEE

We see our completeness in Christ in the pages of the Bible.

Read Psalm 119:165. What does this verse tell us about the Bible's connection to peace? _____
_____
_____
_____

Abundant peace belongs to those who love Your instruction; nothing makes them stumble (Ps. 119:165).

> "When the Spirit of truth comes, He will guide you into all the truth. For He will not speak on His own, but He will speak whatever He hears. He will also declare to you what is to come" (John 16:13).

THIRD—WE UNDERSTAND

Our understanding is not something we have to work at. The Spirit gives it to us.

Read John 16:13.

The job of the Spirit is to g_____ us into all the t_____.

As the Spirit controls our "souled out" minds, He gives us understanding about being complete in Christ.

FOURTH—WE BELIEVE

Our faith is not our own doing. Jesus Himself enables us to believe. He gives us the faith we need as a free gift.

> By grace you are saved through faith, and this is not from yourselves; it is God's gift (Eph. 2:8).

Read Ephesians 2:8. What does this verse say about faith?
- ☐ You need to have it.
- ☐ It is a gift of God.
- ☐ It is hard work.
- ☐ It comes under trial.

When the Spirit controls our minds, we then see, understand, and believe something pretty awesome.

> In Him [Jesus] the entire fullness of God's nature dwells bodily, and you have been filled by Him, who is the head over every ruler and authority (Col. 2:9-10).

Read Colossians 2:9-10. What is it that you will believe?
- ☐ I have been filled by Christ.
- ☐ Christ is the way to peace.
- ☐ Peace can be found.
- ☐ I am not worthy of God.

Do you get it? Since Jesus is now in you, and since Jesus is complete, you can now be complete.

Peace of mind can be accomplished by three acts—surrender, renewal, and warfare. However, it is not us doing these things. It is Him doing them in us. Basically, all we do is ask Him to work.

2-STEP ONE: SURRENDER

In your pursuit of peace, it is absolutely essential that you allow your mind to be souled out—totally consumed by Him. Without that taking place, there will be no completeness, no soundness, and no good welfare in your mind.

On Day 1 of Chapter 2 you will learn about renewal and warfare. For now we are going to focus on the first step to peace of mind—surrender.

In a war when someone surrenders, they are saying, "You win." In the spiritual sense when we surrender to God, we are saying, "I can't, but You can." We admit that we cannot control our minds or make our minds think about good things.

Look at Romans 7:18. What was Paul's conclusion on the matter of doing good (even controlling his mind)?
- ☐ **He wanted to do right, but couldn't.**
- ☐ **He didn't care about doing right.**
- ☐ **He didn't know what right was.**
- ☐ **He couldn't care less about right and wrong.**

I know that nothing good lives in me, that is, in my flesh. For the desire to do what is good is with me, but there is no ability to do it (Rom. 7:18).

To surrender, we give up. We stop trying, and we let Him do it.

When you surrender, pray something like this to God, "Jesus, I believe I have Your mind. But it appears that I, not You, am controlling my mind right now. So by faith, I'm turning it over to You. I can't control it, but You can. Control my mind right now."

3-THE MIND AT PEACE

Right now you need to ask yourself, *Is my mind at peace?* Do I see, understand, and believe that I am complete in Christ?

Ask yourself the following questions. Check all that you would answer yes.
- ☐ **Do I worry about the future?**
- ☐ **Am I concerned about what people think of me?**
- ☐ **Do I get uptight witnessing or sharing a testimony?**
- ☐ **Do I have a hard time tithing?**
- ☐ **Do I think evil or immoral thoughts?**

Who has known the Lord's mind, that he may instruct Him? But we have the mind of Christ (1 Cor. 2:16).

If you checked any of these, it is because you don't have peace of mind … yet. The key steps for you to take right now are to (1) start believing that you are already complete in Christ, and (2) start believing what 1 Corinthians 2:16 says.

"We have the m_____ of Christ."

As you go along in this study, you will learn more about allowing your mind to be totally controlled by Christ through surrender, renewal, and warfare.

4-TALK ABOUT PEACE

1. What is the key to pursuing peace in the mind?
2. What does it mean to you to allow the Spirit to control your mind?
3. What does it mean to you to surrender your mind to Christ?
4. After this week's study, do you sense that your mind is under Christ's control and do you have peace in your mind right now? Explain.

1. *Blue Letter Bible.* "Dictionary and Word Search for 'shalowm (Strong's 07965)' and 'shalam (Strong's 07999)'". Blue Letter Bible. 1996-2002. 25 Feb 2004. <http://www.blueletterbible.org/cgi-bin/words.pl?word=07965&page=1> <http://www.blueletterbible.org/cgi-bin/words.pl?word=07999&page=1>.
2. *Blue Letter Bible.* "Dictionary and Word Search for 'eirene (Strong's 1515)'". Blue Letter Bible. 1996-2002. 25 Feb 2004. <http://www.blueletterbible.org/cgi-bin/words.pl?word=1515&page=1>.
3. *Blue Letter Bible.* "Dictionary and Word Search for 'radaph (Strong's 07291)'". Blue Letter Bible. 1996-2002. 25 Feb 2004. <http://www.blueletterbible.org/cgi-bin/words.pl?word=07291&page=1>.

CHAPTER 2

FROM THE RUT TO REST

Real peace is elusive. And yet, God desires for us as Christians to have inner peace and outer peace. The way God brings peace to us in all of life's difficult situations is by teaching us to move out of the way. When we do that and then allow Him to control our souls, we will find peace, which we so desperately seek.

MEMORY VERSE

"Come to Me, all you who are weary and burdened, and I will give you rest" (Matt. 11:28).

The Big Picture

This week you will continue your study of peace, picking up where you left off last week. As you study you will discover the following:
☐ How to break out from the "up-and-down" Christian life.
☐ The secret to peace with fellow Christians.
☐ How to have peace over fears.
☐ Why witnessing is all about sharing peace.
☐ How to enter into a peaceful rest.

As you read and study, begin with prayer. Remember that it is God who teaches truth. He desires to teach you so that you can, by faith, turn your life over to Him.

Scripture

This week memorize and meditate on Matthew 11:28.

For your private devotional reading this week, finish reading the Book of Ephesians.
Day 1—Ephesians 4:1-8
Day 2—Ephesians 4:9-16
Day 3—Ephesians 4:17-32
Day 4—Ephesians 5:1-14
Day 5—Ephesians 5:15-33
Day 6—Ephesians 6:1-9
Day 7—Ephesians 6:10-24

Prayer Thought

A prayer thought is a short prayer you carry with you in your mind to remain focused on God. You can say your prayer thought to God over and over again. This week make this your prayer thought: *Living God, control my thoughts. May Your thoughts become my thoughts.*

✸ DAY 1: OUT OF THE RUT

Judy had an up-and-down personality. You never could tell what kind of mood she was going to be in. One day she would be sky high, full of excitement and joy. Then the next day she would barely talk and just sulk around all day. Her friends even gave her a nickname, "Moody Judy."

Some folks would try to fix Judy's problem with prescription drugs designed to regulate mood swings, but Judy's problem was spiritual in nature. She was caught in the confession trap. If you've been a Christian long, you might have been caught in the same trap.

1-STEP ONE: SURRENDER

Last week you studied about the first step in controlling your mind—surrender. When you surrender, you admit to God that you have been controlling your own mind but you now desire for Him to control your mind.

This first step is basically a step of confession. Confession is a tremendous place to start allowing Christ to control your mind. However, if you do not move beyond this step, it can become a trap. Why? Because you will soon find yourself taking control of your mind again and then surrendering or confessing again; and your life will become a vicious cycle—sin, confession, sin, confession, sin, confession.

The problem is that living this way will eventually rob you of your joy and kill any peace of mind you have. This is especially true if the sin is the same sin. You feel good after you confess; but then when you commit the same sin again you feel terrible, even worse than before.

As a dog returns to its vomit, so a fool repeats his foolishness (Prov. 26:11).

Read Proverbs 26:11. How does this verse describe a person who commits the same sin over and over? _____

_____

_____

_____

_____

I do not do the good that I want to do, but I practice the evil that I do not want to do (Rom. 7:19).

Paul surely felt that way when he confessed in Romans 7:19.

> "I do not do the g_____ that I want to do, but I p_____ the e_____ that I do not want to do."

The reason Judy was so moody and the reason we all get caught in the confession trap is that we don't take the other steps necessary for our minds to be controlled by Christ.

2-STEP TWO: RENEWAL

After we have gone before God and surrendered our minds to Him, we tend to think that we are finished. However, it is in the next step, renewal, where we will really begin to gain peace of mind.

Sometimes we need a library book for a longer period of time, so we renew our due date. This means we get a fresh start on having the book. At times, our minds need a fresh start, a renewing. We have surrendered, but then we need to ask God to renew our minds.

Do not be conformed to this age, but be transformed by the renewing of your mind, so that you may discern what is the good, pleasing, and perfect will of God (Rom. 12:2).

Read Romans 12:2. What did Paul appeal to people to do?

> "Be t_____ by the r_____ of your mind."

Transformed means "to be changed." In this case it means to be changed back to the way we were when we first came to faith in Christ.

Therefore as you have received Christ Jesus the Lord, walk in Him (Col. 2:6).

Read Colossians 2:6. What does this verse tell us about our walk with Jesus?
☐ We need to try harder to follow Jesus.
☐ We walk the same way as when we received Him.
☐ Walking with Jesus is difficult.
☐ Only the good walk with Jesus.

When your mind is renewed, you get a fresh start. In a sense, it is like you are starting out brand-new, like when you first came to Christ. When you go back and are renewed like this, you are souled out— you have peace in your mind as it is under His control.

Going back, starting over, and being renewed is all the work of the Spirit. The Spirit does this work when you allow Him to work. Pray something like this: "Living God, renew my mind. Take me back to the way it was when I first trusted You. Control my mind. Make my mind new in Christ."

3-STEP THREE: WARFARE

Even when your mind is surrendered and renewed, there is a war going on between God and Satan. Since God is inside of you, you are thrust into that war. The war often is fought in your mind as Satan, using your sinful nature, brings attacks on your mind. These attacks will certainly destroy any peace in your mind unless you learn to defend your mind against Satan's attacks.

Defense must start with the armor of God found in Ephesians 6:10-18. Read this passage in your Bible. What are the different pieces of the armor?_____

_____

_____

_____

Of primary importance are the:
- Helmet of Salvation – This means our minds are surrounded by our knowledge of our own salvation.
- Gospel of Peace – The gospel brings peace of mind because we are now sure of our standing with God.
- Shield of Faith – By faith He lives, not me. (See Gal. 2:20.) We allow Him to do the fighting, not us.

What can you do to have these three pieces of armor protecting you from the war with Satan? Read verse 11 of Ephesians 6.

What does this verse say to do?_____

_____

_____

Put on the full armor of God so that you can stand against the tactics of the Devil (Eph. 6:11).

From the Rut to Rest

You put on invisible things by faith through prayer. You pray, "God, right now I ask You to clothe me with this armor. I believe I am a child of God. Surround my mind with this knowledge that I am a Christian. I know that there is peace between You and me because the gospel is the good news that You love me. I ask You to live through me right now. Do the fighting for me; it is You, not me fighting against Satan and the flesh."

4-TALK ABOUT PEACE

1. Have you ever been like Judy, caught in the trap of confessing the same sins over and over again?
2. What does it mean to you to renew your mind, and how does that happen?
3. How have you been involved in spiritual warfare in the past?
4. What have you learned today that will aid you in the pursuit of peace?

✸ DAY 2: PEACE AMONG BROTHERS

Two students in the youth group, Sean and Kenn, just could not get along. The bad thing was they were the two main leaders of the group. Then a weird thing happened. They were both assigned to serve as leaders for the same children's Bible club. Amazingly these two, who had been at each others throats for years, found peace and even friendship. What was it that brought them together?

1-GOOD AND PLEASANT

We have established that peace is both inward and outward. Outward peace is when unity and harmony exist between people.

How good and pleasant it is when brothers can live together! It is like fine oil on the head (Ps. 133:1-2).

Read Psalm 133:1-2a. What does it say about brothers living in unity?
- ☐ It is a good thing.
- ☐ It is only natural.
- ☐ It cannot be seen.
- ☐ It takes many people to create peace.

In verse 2, peace among brothers is compared to what?

_____

When you read about "fine oil," you probably have no clue what David was referring to. In Exodus 30:22-33, we see that this oil actually was a God-given blend of spices and was designated as "holy oil." In fact, the oil was so holy that Exodus 30:33 tells us what is to happen to anyone making oil like this on his own.

What this means is that peace among brothers is holy and can only be made by God. People making peace on their own will fail.

Read Psalm 133:3. What else is peace among brothers compared to? _____

_____
_____
_____
_____
_____
_____
_____

Dew from Mount Hermon was excessive. So excessive, in fact, that it resembled a heavy rain most mornings. And Mount Hermon's peak held snow year-round. In the arid country, this dew was considered a refreshing blessing.

Read Hebrews 12:22. What is Mount Zion in this verse?
☐ **The biggest mountain in Israel**
☐ **The home of the Jebusites**
☐ **Heaven**
☐ **A rare mountain with no top**

Mount Zion is the heavenly city, or heaven itself. What this simile means is that peace among brothers will be a refreshing blessing (dew) in heaven (Mount Zion).

"Anyone who blends something like it or puts some of it on an unauthorized person must be cut off from his people" (Ex. 30:33).

It is like the dew of Hermon falling on the mountains of Zion. For there the LORD has appointed the blessing— life forevermore (Ps. 133:3).

You have come to Mount Zion, to the city of the living God (the heavenly Jerusalem), to myriads of angels in festive gathering (Heb. 12:22).

Brothers, I was not able to speak to you as spiritual people but as people of the flesh, as babies in Christ. I fed you milk, not solid food, because you were not yet able to receive it. In fact, you are still not able, because you are still fleshly. For since there is envy and strife among you, are you not fleshly and living like ordinary people?
(1 Cor. 3:1-3).

"I am in them and You are in me. May they be made completely one, so that the world may know You sent Me and that You have loved them just as You have loved Me"
(John 17:23).

2-WHERE THERE IS NO PEACE

Probably the greatest hindrance to the church today is the lack of unity, or lack of peace.

Read 1 Corinthians 3:1-3. What did Paul call these people? Check all that apply.
☐ **Fleshly**
☐ **Babies**
☐ **Ordinary people**
☐ **Nicolaitans**

Paul was not pleased with the church at Corinth because they showed a total lack of unity with no peace. John 17:23 shows Jesus' concern for His followers.

According to John 17:23, what did Jesus desire for His followers?
_____
_____
_____

The result of unity would be that the world would know Jesus was sent by God. When there is no unity among brothers, as in Corinth, it seems only natural to the world to judge the church and reach a shocking conclusion: Jesus is not God's Son.

Think about it. If the world, including the non-Christians at school, look and see no unity in your youth group, they can conclude that Jesus is not God's Son.

3-THE FOUNDATION OF OUTER PEACE

In our pursuit, we will find there are three principles to outer peace.

Flee from youthful passions, and pursue righteousness, faith, love, and peace, along with those who call on the Lord from a pure heart (2 Tim. 2:22).

PRINCIPLE ONE: THE PRINCIPLE OF COMMUNITY
At the beginning of this pursuit, we see something simple yet profound. What does 2 Timothy 2:22 say about our pursuit of outer peace?
☐ **It is done by a group of people.**
☐ **It is rarely effective.**
☐ **It follows after church membership.**
☐ **The key is consent.**

Amazingly, Paul told Timothy to run after peace with others also running after peace. In other words, if you are the only one looking for outer peace, it won't happen. Your church, your youth group, and/or your friends must also be pursuing unity.

PRINCIPLE TWO: THE PRINCIPLE OF PURPOSE

The greatest example of a group of people living in peace and unity is found in Acts 2:42-47. These early Christians were united with common purposes.

Read the verses in your Bible. What were the common purposes?
- ☐ **Teaching**
- ☐ **Fellowship**
- ☐ **Worship**
- ☐ **Outreach**

Actually, we can see all these things working in this group. The common purposes were so evident that people even sold their possessions and shared everything with each other.

PRINCIPLE THREE: THE PRINCIPLE OF SALT

Read Mark 9:50. What does this verse say about peace? Check all that apply.
- ☐ **Christians should be salt.**
- ☐ **Salt is needed for peace.**
- ☐ **Salt is needed only for meat.**
- ☐ **Most salt is good for nothing.**

"Salt is good, but if the salt should lose its flavor, how can you make it salty? Have salt among yourselves and be at peace with one another" (Mark 9:50).

From this verse you can see that Christians are to be salt and that salt is necessary for peace. The obvious question then becomes, "What exactly is salt, and how do Christians get salt?"

Salt is necessary for life and is used as a preservative for food. Likewise, Christians are a source of spiritual life for the world when we allow Christ to direct our paths.

The principle of salt means that for there to be peace among brothers, all the brothers (principle one) must pursue a common goal (principle two). Unity comes from having Christ in us (principle three), not us trying to bring unity.

4-TALK ABOUT PEACE

1. In what way is the "principle of community" at work in your youth group? Do you really share things?
2. In what way is the "principle of purpose" at work in your youth group? What are your common goals?
3. Is Jesus working in your youth group as "salt"? If so, how?
4. Since you can't make real peace among your friends, how will peace ever come?

✺ DAY 3: PEACE OVER FEAR

In my mind I understood that I was complete in Christ. I also understood how to keep my mind focused on Christ. But when two of the teens on my mission team had suddenly disappeared in downtown Cairo, Egypt, I had no peace. All I had was fear and trembling. What had gone wrong? How could peace have so easily left me? Well, I had crossed over from mind to emotions; and my emotions were not controlled by Christ, but by fear.

1-THE FEAR FACTOR

Have you ever been totally at peace, but then a terrible or frightening situation hit, and suddenly you had no peace at all? If so, you know that circumstances can rob you of inner peace.

How did the disciples respond to the situation in Mark 6:47-50?

_____

_____

The disciples lost their peace because of fear, the fear of death. What are the things that you fear most? _____

_____

_____

And he said, "I heard You in the garden, and I was afraid because I was naked, so I hid" (Gen. 3:10).

As long as we have fears, our inner peace is at best temporary. Yet everyone has some fears. Why? Well, to begin with, we inherited fear from Adam. Read Genesis 3:10.

Adam was a_____ and so he h_____.

Obviously, Adam was not a man with much peace. And that fear has been passed down to each generation.

Read Luke 2:10. What was the first thing the angels said when Jesus was born?

"Do not be a_____."

You might be wondering why the angel told people not to be afraid. Man's emotions by nature are fearful. Even the bravest (if not controlled by Christ) has a soul with fearful emotions.

Why do the emotions of a Christian fear the unknown? It is because even though in our minds we know we are complete in Christ (therefore at peace), our minds often do not translate this to our emotions. Emotions are there acting not out of faith, but out of the natural order of things. So when certain situations arise, the emotions go crazy; and fear replaces peace in our souls. Then our circumstances, not faith, carry the day.

2-COOL IN THE FURNACE

So when frightening circumstances arise that hit at our emotions, how do we have peace and not fear?

We can find the answer by looking at the situation that Shadrach, Meshach, and Abednego faced. Read Daniel 3:16-18. In these verses, we see Shadrach, Meshach, and Abednego's response when told they were going to be thrown into a fiery furnace. Obviously, these guys were at perfect peace in a terrifying situation.

What was it that gave them peace at this time? _____
_____
_____
_____
_____

FIRST: THEIR EMOTIONS HAD BEEN OVERRIDDEN
In verse 16, they said...

"We don't n_____ to g_____ you an a_____."

The angel said to them, "Do not be afraid, for you see, I announce to you good news of great joy that will be for all the people" (Luke 2:10).

Shadrach, Meshach, and Abednego replied to the king, "Nebuchadnezzar, we don't need to give you an answer to this question. If the God we serve exists, then He can rescue us from the furnace of blazing fire, and He can rescue us from the power of you, the king. But even if He does not rescue us, we want you as king to know that we will not serve your gods or worship the gold statue you set up" (Dan. 3:16-18).

From the Rut to Rest

How do you respond when someone threatens you? More than likely you go on the offensive. Why? Striking back is an emotional response to fear. Someone calls you a name; you call them a name back. That isn't peace!

But Shadrach and the boys did not try to defend themselves. Why? Basically, the normal emotions present in most human beings were not ruling these boys' lives. Their emotions were not in control of their lives.

SECOND: FAITH WAS IN CONTROL
In verse 17, we see what had overridden these guys' emotions. It was faith.

What did they testify about God in verse 17? _____
_____
_____
_____
_____
_____
_____
_____
_____

Think about it for a minute. These guys believed something that was completely impossible. They believed that God would rescue them from the fiery furnace. They did not doubt; they believed.

THIRD: BY FAITH, THEY LIVED THEIR CONVICTIONS
Look at verse 18. What did they state about how they lived their lives?
☐ **They let circumstances determine their course of action.**
☐ **They let emotions determine their course of action.**
☐ **They let convictions determine their course of action.**
☐ **They let each day have its due.**

These guys were controlled by faith, not emotions. By faith, they lived out their convictions. They knew God's truths to be true. In this case, the boys knew worship was reserved for God, and by faith they were not going to worship an image of gold.

3-PURSUING EMOTIONAL PEACE

Shadrach, Meshach, and Abednego had emotional peace in a most trying circumstance because their emotions were overridden by faith. They lived out their convictions by faith.

But how do we do that? Where do we start? We start by allowing faith to take precedence over our emotions. This is not something that we do. We can't just say, "Faith, take over my emotions." There are two practical steps to allowing God to override your emotions with faith.

STEP ONE: SURRENDER
Just as you allowed God to control your mind by surrendering your mind to Him, in the same way you surrender your emotions to Him. You say, "God, I cannot control these emotions, but You can. Take all my emotions and totally control them. I am out of here."

This surrender of your emotions is part of what worship is all about—bowing down before God and turning your emotional heart over to Him.

STEP TWO: REMOVAL
If you desire for your emotions to be overridden by faith, you need to remove your emotions from planet earth. Actually, the three boys had already done this. Their hearts were already in heaven. Well, guess what? Your heart is already in heaven, too. Read Colossians 3:1-2.

You can't do it. You can't make your emotions abide in heaven. But God has already done it. Now it's just a matter of faith. Go to God and pray, "Living God, my emotions are with You. Let me seek You and seek what is above. Let me desire what You desire."

You can pray this only if He is living through you. In your own emotions, you desire things of this earth. By faith, He now lives, not you. You are souled out.

Our desires give way to His desire. Just like Shad and the boys, our heart is removed to heaven; and we have peace, not fear. Emotional peace becomes reality when faith overrides your emotions, and by faith you live your convictions.

So if you have been raised with the Messiah, seek what is above, where the Messiah is, seated at the right hand of God. Set your minds on what is above, not on what is on the earth (Col. 3:1-2).

4-TALK ABOUT PEACE

1. What are circumstances that rob you of peace?
2. What does it mean to you to have faith override your emotions?
3. Why is it important to surrender and remove your emotions in order to have emotional peace?
4. Do you believe you can be at peace emotionally even in a difficult or dangerous situation?

⊛ DAY 4: GIVING AWAY PEACE

 Most people didn't understand Todd. You see, wherever Todd went he did just one thing—he told people about Jesus. They called him "preacher man" or "evangelist" or "Jesus freak." Yet Todd never worried what they said about him; he was controlled by a higher power. The week before graduation, the people Todd had led to Christ threw him a surprise party. There were 27 people at that party, and 26 of them were there because one guy had allowed Jesus to live through him.

1-THE GOSPEL OF PEACE

When you really start to think about the gospel of Jesus Christ, you begin to realize that it is the gospel of peace. Remember, inner peace is completeness, and outer peace is unity. When someone receives Christ, that person is now both complete in Him and in union with Him.

The beginning of the gospel of Jesus Christ, the Son of God (Mark 1:1).

In Mark 1:1, we see the purpose of the Book of Mark. What is that purpose? Check all that apply.
- ☐ To supplement our knowledge
- ☐ To explain the life of Jesus
- ☐ To tell us how to live
- ☐ To tell the beginning of the gospel about Jesus, the Son of God

Some people have said that the word *gospel* means "true." But the word *gospel* in Greek means "news of victory."[1] So what is the victory that the good news is about? Read Luke 4:17-19. Jesus tells us in this passage about some "news of victory."

What has been gained in this victory? Check all that apply.
☐ **Freedom for captives**
☐ **Sight for the blind**
☐ **Release for the oppressed**
☐ **God's favor for all**

Do you get it? This is speaking about you and me. The war is a war between two great sides. On one side is the side of sin where Satan reigns. The other side is the side of God. Sin and Satan held us captive, blinded us to the truth about God, and oppressed us.

In fact, what does Romans 5:10 call us?

e_____ of God

When Jesus came and preached the "gospel," He was preaching good news about a great victory to be won at the cross. There, Jesus defeated sin and Satan for all time, and we are no longer enemies of God.

2-SHARING PEACE = SHARING THE GOSPEL

The reason we are often unconcerned or even afraid to share the gospel is that we do not realize that we have good news of a great victory and that peace is now available.

Read Ephesians 2:17. This verse is talking about Jesus. What was the message He preached? _____
_____
_____
_____
_____
_____
_____
_____

> The scroll of the prophet Isaiah was given to Him, and unrolling the scroll, He found the place where it was written: "The Spirit of the Lord is upon Me, because He has anointed Me to preach good news to the poor. He has sent Me to proclaim freedom to the captives and recovery of sight to the blind, to set free the oppressed, to proclaim the year of the Lord's favor" (Luke 4:17-19).

> For if, while we were enemies, we were reconciled to God through the death of His Son, then how much more, having been reconciled, will we be saved by His life! (Rom. 5:10).

> When Christ came, He proclaimed the good news of peace to you who were far away and peace to those who were near (Eph. 2:17).

> Because all the fullness was pleased to dwell in Him, and to reconcile everything to Himself through Him by making peace through the blood of His cross—whether things on earth or things in heaven (Col. 1:19-20).

> "Whatever house you enter, first say, 'Peace to this household'" (Luke 10:5).

Jesus preached a message of peace. Obviously, that involved peace between people. However, the greatest peace He preached was peace with God. He preached this not just with words. Read Colossians 1:19-20.

When Jesus sent His disciples out on a mission to preach the gospel, He gave them unusual instructions. What did He tell them to do in Luke 10:5 when they came to the household of a stranger?

☐ Say, "Peace to this household."
☐ Ask the man of the house for a word of prayer.
☐ Seek a house belonging to a prophet.
☐ Follow a peaceful man to his home.

A greeting of "peace to this household" was a greeting which stood for the "shalom" of the Messiah. In other words, greeting the household with "peace to you" meant greeting them with the promise of the coming Messiah.

What this means is that the disciples were to tell each household they came to that they were the messengers of the Messiah and that peace with God was now available to all. (Peace with God = salvation.) Salvation was available if the person was willing to receive this "good news" of the "victory" over sin, Satan, and even death.

3-AMBASSADORS OF PEACE
What does 2 Corinthians 5:20 call us?

> Therefore, we are ambassadors for Christ; certain that God is appealing through us, we plead on Christ's behalf, "Be reconciled to God" (2 Cor. 5:20).

"a_____ for C_____"

As an ambassador, what is the message we bring from the One we represent?

"Be r_____ to G_____."

As ambassadors, we have one job: to represent Christ. As ambassadors, we have one message: be reconciled to God (through faith in Christ). As ambassadors, we visibly represent Christ in many ways, and we proclaim this message in many ways.

Read Ephesians 4:4-8. What does this passage tell us about unity and diversity? _____
_____
_____
_____

There are many parts to the body of Christ and many different ways the message is spread. But there is one job—being an ambassador; and there is one message—be reconciled to God.

What about you? What do you think your role as an ambassador involves? In other words, where and how is God leading you to tell the message? _____
_____
_____
_____

> There is one body and one Spirit, just as you were called to one hope at your calling; one Lord, one faith, one baptism, one God and Father of all, who is above all and through all and in all. Now grace was given to each one of us according to the measure of the Messiah's gift. For it says: When He ascended on high, … He gave gifts to people (Eph. 4:4-8).

Remember this: you are only an ambassador, and your job is to let Christ live through you. On your own you don't witness, serve, minister, or do anything.

4-TALK ABOUT PEACE

1. In your life do you think the gospel is really a gospel of peace?
2. When you witness, are you really sharing about peace?
3. As an ambassador, what is your job?
4. If you are an ambassador of peace, to whom have you been sent?

✦ DAY 5: REST

J.D. quit Christianity. Well … he quit going to church and he said he was tired of Sunday School. Then one day his Sunday School teacher visited J.D. to talk about why he wasn't coming. When J.D. said he was tired of church, the teacher told J.D. that he needed a "rest." J.D. agreed, and then the teacher explained how Christians are to truly rest. Now J.D. is in worship every week and is not weary anymore.

From the Rut to Rest

1-WHAT IS REST?

To understand rest, let's look at the three main words for *rest* in the New Testament.

KATAPAUSIS – THE RESTING PLACE

Katapausis is used primarily in the Book of Hebrews. It refers to a place and a state where we rest.[2]

ANAPAUSIS – REST FROM WEARINESS

Anapausis is used by Jesus in Matthew. It means to refresh someone or to recharge them.[3]

SABBATISMOS – REST FROM WORK

Sabbatismos refers to the Sabbath rest. It was a day when people were not allowed to work.[4]

So what do all these different words tell us about rest? Rest is not just doing nothing; it is God's way of dealing with a basic human problem.

We try to do the work of living this life ourselves. Obviously, this is a losing situation. But we forget what we are supposed to do—be out of the way, souled out, allowing Him to do the work.

Do you remember that one of the keys to peace of mind was surrender? When we enter into the rest God has for us, we come to a place of surrender.

> I know that nothing good lives in me, that is, in my flesh. For the desire to do what is good is with me, but there is no ability to do it (Rom. 7:18).

Read Romans 7:18. What hope do we have of peace in and of ourselves?_____

_____

2-REST FROM WEARINESS

If you are spiritually weary, guess what? You won't be at peace. Guess what else? Jesus doesn't want you to be that way.

> "Come to Me, all you who are weary and burdened, and I will give you rest" (Matt. 11:28).

Read Matthew 11:28. Who is Jesus addressing in this passage?

_____

Where are the weary to go? _____

What will He do in return? _____
_____

This is a simple process. His job is to give rest. Our job is to come to Him. The process is as easy as one, two, three.

FIRST: WE TAKE HIS YOKE.
A lot of people think this means we get busy doing His work. But that is not His yoke!

The Jews of Jesus' day were under a heavy yoke; it was called the law. The law spelled out hundreds of things a person was to do and not do. It was impossible to keep all of the law. Jesus came and brought a new yoke; it was called relationship. The Jews never imagined much of a relationship with God; they had too much to worry about in keeping the law. But Jesus invited people to come, not to laws or teaching, but according to verse 28, to Him.

Abundant peace belongs to those who love Your instruction; nothing makes them stumble (Ps. 119:165).

SECOND: WE LEARN FROM HIM.
Read Psalm 119:165. What do those who love God's instruction have? _____

Why do these people have peace? Read Psalm 119:66.

    They ask God to t_____ them.

Teach me good judgment and discernment, for I rely on Your commands (Ps. 119:66).

Do you see? He teaches us. He uses the Word to teach us. According to Jeremiah 31:33, what does He do?

    He w_____ it on our h_____.

THIRD: WE FIND REST.
The rest we find is *anapausis,* rest from weariness. Here is how it all comes together. We have the Holy Spirit living inside of us. When we read the Bible, He starts to teach our hearts. As He teaches our hearts, we are at rest. We are rejuvenated. God's Spirit makes us complete; since we are complete, we are at peace.

"Instead, this is the covenant I will make with the house of Israel after those days"—the LORD's declaration. "I will place My law within them and write it on their hearts. I will be their God, and they will be My people" (Jer. 31:33).

Some practical applications are appropriate at this point:
- We COME to Christ in prayer.
- We TAKE His yoke. This step implies first receiving Christ and then allowing Him to be our life.
- We LEARN from Him. This step implies studying His Word.
- We ALLOW Him to bring us rest.

3-REST FROM WORK

One of the main problems with trying to work your way into heaven by being good is that you never know if you are being good enough. You can't have inner peace, inner completeness, because you always feel you are lacking something. *If I had just witnessed to that girl. If I had just been nicer to that guy.* You know the drill.

But God wants to give you peace of mind knowing that you are complete in Christ. God wants your mind to be controlled by the Spirit so that you will see, understand, and believe that you are already complete. To do this, He provides a place for you to rest.

God's plan was always that people should not work their way to Him, but instead rest.

> A Sabbath rest remains, therefore, for God's people. For the person who has entered His rest has rested from his own work, just as God did from His (Heb. 4:9-10).

Read Hebrews 4:9-10. What is available for God's people?

A S_____ r_____.

The Sabbath rest, the *sabbatismos,* is a rest from work.

According to Hebrews 4:10, what happens as we enter God's rest?
- ☐ We sit around in recliners.
- ☐ We learn the words to all our songs.
- ☐ We rest from all our work.
- ☐ We dance.

What does it mean when we rest from all our work? Does it mean we just stop doing everything? No, it means we understand our position as complete in Christ. Then we take a big breath and rest and let Him take over doing everything. We have just entered the place of rest.

4-TALK ABOUT PEACE

1. In what ways do you still try to do good works for God?
2. What is His yoke, and have you taken it up?
3. When God rested, He didn't stop working. What do you believe He is now going to do through you?
4. If you believe that you are now complete in Christ, how can you rest in that belief?

1. *Theological Dictionary of the New Testament*, s.v. "gospel."
2. *Blue Letter Bible.* "Lexicon and Strong's Concordance Search for 2663". Blue Letter Bible. 1996-2002. 25 Feb 2004. <*http://www.blueletterbible.org/cgi-bin/strongs.pl?strongs=2663&page=1*>.
3. *Vine's Expository Dictionary of New Testament Words*, s.v. "rest."
4. *Blue Letter Bible.* "Dictionary and Word Search for 'sabbatismos (Strong's 4520)'". Blue Letter Bible. 1996-2002. 25 Feb 2004. <*http://www.blueletterbible.org/cgi-bin/words.pl?word=4520&page=1*>.

CHAPTER 3

GOD'S OFFER OF JOY

When you are no longer running your own life, God will bring peace to your mind. Peace is produced when the Spirit is in control. Peace is primarily a thing that takes place in the mind. In the emotions, God desires for us to experience the fruit of joy. When the Spirit is controlling us and we are souled out, we will find real joy.

The Big Picture

This week you will discover the following:
- [ ] Why God has given us emotions
- [ ] The nature of joy.
- [ ] How God offers us joy.
- [ ] What we have to do to find joy.
- [ ] Why good times do not bring joy.

As you read these pages, begin each day with prayer. Ask God to teach you about joy. Ask God to make joy a reality in your life. Allow Him to change you this week.

MEMORY VERSE

"I have spoken these things to you so that My joy may be in you and your joy may be complete" (John 15:11).

Scripture

This week memorize and meditate on John 15:11.

For your private devotional reading this week, read John 15–17.
Day 1—John 15:1-17
Day 2—John 15:18-27
Day 3—John 16:1-15
Day 4—John 16:16-33
Day 5—John 17:1-5
Day 6—John 17:6-19
Day 7—John 17:20-26

As you read, notice how often Jesus talked about joy as He was nearing the cross.

Prayer Thought

As you go about your schedule this week, keep this prayer in your thoughts: *Let me see Your glory, Lord, Your glory.*

✷ DAY 1: EMOTIONS

If there was ever a man in the Bible who should have had great joy, it was King Saul. After all, he had a great family, he was king, and his kingdom was expanding. But Saul was a man of sorrow and torment. He tried unsuccessfully to kill his servant David, whom he wrongly assumed was his enemy. He even tried to turn his own son against David. When all else failed to bring him happiness, he turned to a witch for help. Eventually Saul's life ended tragically.

Why did Saul's life go so sour? Why could Saul not find any joy in being the first king in the history of Israel? The problem went back to an event in Saul's life (see 1 Sam. 15) where Saul failed to follow God's specific instructions. Saul was living for himself, not God. And when that happened, Saul never again saw the glory of God working in his life or in the world around him.

1–SOME BACKGROUND

If you are a Christian, Christ is in you. Yet He may not be in control! Your desire should be to be souled out—to have a soul controlled by Him. Allowing Jesus to control your soul means He controls your mind, emotions, and will.

Read John 3:27-30. What gave John the Baptist joy?
- ☐ **The weekend**
- ☐ **Being well known**
- ☐ **The opportunity to serve**
- ☐ **The groom's voice**

It gave John joy just to hear Jesus. That is why he said in verse 30 …

> "He must i_____, but I must d_____."

2–WHY WE HAVE EMOTIONS

Emotions can really mess up our relationships with others and our relationship with God. One reason is that emotions seem unpredictable and are so easily swayed by even the slightest thing.

John responded, "No one can receive a single thing unless it's given to him from heaven. You yourselves can testify that I said, 'I am not the Messiah, but I've been sent ahead of Him.' He who has the bride is the groom. But the groom's friend, who stands by and listens for him, rejoices greatly at the groom's voice. So this joy of mine is complete. He must increase, but I must decrease" (John 3:27-30).

Read Jonah 4:5-8. What strange thing (v. 6) made Jonah happy?

_____

According to verses 7-8, what made Jonah angry enough to die?
- ☐ He lost his staff
- ☐ The plant died
- ☐ Jonah's wife died
- ☐ A rainy day

If you look at the above answers without reading the passage, you would probably guess the third one, as the other answers are silly. But Jonah became emotionally distraught to the point of not wanting to live because of the death of a plant.

So why would God leave us with something like emotions that can so easily get messed up? He wants us to give our emotions over to Him by faith and allow Him to be the center of our emotional life.

Read Luke 22:44-45. Jesus was in the garden, almost overcome by emotions. He was praying for the Father to control His emotions. But, look at the disciples; they were …

"E_____ from their g_____."

Obviously Jesus' emotions were being controlled by God; the disciple's emotions were not under God's control. That all changed in the Book of Acts.

3-GETTING IN TOUCH WITH YOUR EMOTIONS

Believe it or not, God wants you to get in touch with your feelings. God wants you to know which emotions come from Him and which emotions come from your flesh.

Review the fruit produced by the Spirit in Galatians 5:22-23. It is obvious that joy is an emotion that comes from God. Joy is a feeling, while love, although influenced by emotion, is primarily an action.

Jonah left the city and sat down east of it. He made himself a shelter there and sat in its shade to see what would happen to the city. Then the Lord God appointed a plant, and it grew up to provide shade over Jonah's head to ease his discomfort. Jonah was greatly pleased with the plant. When dawn came the next day, God appointed a worm that attacked the plant, and it withered. As the sun was rising, God appointed a scorching east wind. The sun beat down on Jonah's head so that he almost fainted, and he wanted to die. He said, "It's better for me to die than to live" (Jonah 4:5-8)

Being in anguish, He prayed more fervently, and His sweat became like drops of blood falling to the ground. When He got up from prayer and came to the disciples, He found them sleeping, exhausted from their grief (Luke 22:44-45).

The fruit of the Spirit is love, joy, peace, patience, kindness, goodness, faith, gentleness, self-control (Gal. 5:22-23).

Now the works of the flesh are obvious: sexual immorality, moral impurity, promiscuity, idolatry, sorcery, hatreds, strife, jealousy, outbursts of anger, selfish ambitions, dissensions, factions, envy, drunkenness, carousing, and anything similar (Gal. 5:19-21).

In the same chapter—Galatians 5:19-21—we see some of the works of the flesh. These include ...

h_____, j_____, and e_____ as well as a_____ s_____

So hatred, jealousy, envy, and anything similar are from the flesh.

According to verse 19, the works of the flesh are o_____.

In other words, you pretty much know when your emotions are controlled by the flesh and when they are controlled by the Spirit. As we become aware that our emotions are controlled by the flesh, then we have an opportunity to turn them over to Christ again.

Y-TALK ABOUT JOY

1. What part do your emotions play in affecting your overall soul?
2. Why do you think God left us with emotions in the first place?
3. Why do you think the primary emotion God desires for us is joy?
4. Are you aware of when your emotions are controlled by the flesh? Describe a recent time your emotions were controlled by the flesh.

★ DAY 2: WHAT IS JOY AND WHERE DOES IT COME FROM?

Susan knew there was more to life than what she was experiencing. If you asked her what she wanted, she would say, "to be happy, of course!" Her desire to experience happiness was fairly strong, and right after her high school graduation she set off on a search for happiness.

At first, she sought the happiness she longed for in a guy; but soon that seemed not to bring any true happiness.

Then she turned to hard partying. For a while she felt pretty good inside with alcohol and drugs controlling her senses; but when she flunked out of college, she wasn't happy anymore. As she wandered from job to job, she stumbled across a religious cult. Thinking she had nothing to lose, she joined the cult. It took her three years to discern there was no real joy in that group.

About this time Susan's best friend from high school found a relationship with Jesus Christ. When her friend visited and told her about the joy she had since coming to Christ, Susan became interested. Eventually, Susan found true joy and happiness in a relationship with the Son of God.

1–WHAT IS JOY?

Everybody, just like Susan, wants to have joy in life. But talking to different people, we get different ideas of what joy is. So let's see what you think.

Write your own definition of joy. _____
_____
_____
_____
_____
_____
_____

The best way to understand joy is from a biblical view. In the Old Testament, the main word for *joy* in the Hebrew language is *simchah*, which actually means "to be excited."[1] Thus, we can know that joy means excitement.

In the New Testament the main word is *chara,* which means "to be merry."[2] We can say that joy means our emotions are up. We feel great; we are excited. In slang terms: we are pumped.

We see from the Bible that joy is both outward and inward. A great example of this is found in Mary when Jesus was born. Read Luke 2:10.

The angels brought Good News of g_____ j_____.

The angel said to them, "Do not be afraid, for you see, I announce to you good news of great joy that will be for all the people" (Luke 2:10).

God's Offer of Joy

Mary was treasuring up all these things in her heart and meditating on them (Luke 2:19).

Read Luke 2:19. What did Mary do with the joy, the excitement, the merriness of the birth of Jesus?
☐ She sang a song of joy!
☐ She celebrated with a party.
☐ She meditated on it in her heart.
☐ She proclaimed the goodness of God.

How could Mary possibly keep all this in her heart? Real joy, although it will change outward things, is primarily an inward thing. When Mary kept the joy in her, it in no way diminished the level of her joy. It just shows that joy is not only outward excitement but also inward merriment.

2—WHERE DOES JOY COME FROM?

One of the saddest things about life in the 21st century is that so many want joy in their lives, yet they don't know where to find it.

What are the typical places people look for joy? _____
_____
_____
_____
_____

Searching for joy is not necessarily a bad thing, depending on where one searches. When you see your friends drinking to get joy or when you see your parents spending money to get joy, this just emphasizes that God has made us to seek to have joy in our lives.

All that my eyes desired, I did not deny them. I did not refuse myself any pleasure, for I took pleasure in all my struggles. This was my reward for all my struggles. When I considered all that I had accomplished and what I had labored to achieve, I found everything to be futile and a pursuit of the wind. There was nothing to be gained under the sun (Eccl. 2:10-11).

Read Ecclesiastes 2:10-11. What was this guy (Solomon) looking for? _____
_____
_____

Where did this guy look? _____
_____
_____

What did he find? _____
_____
_____

Read Psalm 16:11. What does God hope that people seeking joy will do?
☐ **Find joy in His presence**
☐ **Find joy in athletics**
☐ **Be miserable**
☐ **Find joy at His right hand**

God is hoping that people seeking joy from the things of this world will abandon that search and instead search for Him. Why?

Read Psalm 4:7. What do we know about joy and God?
☐ **God's joy is greater than the things of this world.**
☐ **God wants people to drink.**
☐ **God is not into joy like we are.**
☐ **Too much joy is not a good thing.**

God wants people to have joy. But He knows that will happen only when they are in Him and He is in them; real joy comes from God.

3-JOY FROM SEEING GOD'S GLORY

As we have seen, joy comes from God. It is when we see God's glory that we begin to have true joy.

Read Romans 5:2b and fill in the blanks below.

"We r_____ in the h_____ of the g_____ of G_____."

What this means is that joy (rejoicing) is a product of the "hope of the glory of God." As we see and experience God's glory, we have the emotion of joy.

There is joy that comes from sources other than seeing God's glory. But since God desires for us to see His glory and give Him glory, He ties our joy directly to our relationship with Him. Joy, therefore, is the primary emotion of any Christian in a relationship with God.

According to Psalm 100:1-2, what does God want us to do when we worship Him? _____

_____

You [God] reveal the path of life to me; in Your presence is abundant joy; in Your right hand are eternal pleasures (Ps. 16:11).

You [God] have put more joy in my heart than they have when their grain and new wine abound (Ps. 4:7).

Through Him, we have obtained access by faith into this grace in which we stand, and we rejoice in the hope of the glory of God (Rom. 5:2).

Shout triumphantly to the LORD, all the earth. Serve the LORD with gladness; come before Him with joyful songs (Ps. 100:1-2).

4—TALK ABOUT JOY

1. How would you describe joy in your life?
2. Where have you looked for joy before?
3. Why do you think God is the source of true joy?
4. What does it mean to you to "see and experience God's glory"?

☀ DAY 3: GOD'S OFFER

The preacher told the congregation that God had a great offer for them—He would give them joy. Rex listened to the sermon; but when the time came to respond to the offer, Rex was afraid. After all, what if it didn't work? Then what would he do? Sadly Rex rejected God's offer and left unchanged.

1—HOW JOY WILL CHANGE YOU

You should not be surprised to learn that joy can have a tremendous impact on your life.

JOY CHANGES YOUR STRENGTH
Read Nehemiah 8:10. What does Nehemiah tell the people?

> "Your strength comes from r_____ in the L_____."

What this means is that when someone sees God's glory, the person has great joy—the joy of the Lord. This joy then strengthens that person for all of the difficulties he or she faces in life. Think about how having God's joy can change your strength.

JOY CHANGES YOUR APPEARANCE
Read Proverbs 15:13. What does a joyful heart do? _____
_____

People with the joy of God in their hearts are outwardly cheerful. This is not an act. They reflect what is inside of them. Over time, people who experience joy will look better than people consumed with anger, envy, jealousy, and so forth.

Then he said to them, "Go and eat what is rich, drink what is sweet, and send portions to those who have nothing prepared, since today is holy to our Lord. Do not grieve, because your strength comes from rejoicing in the LORD" (Neh. 8:10).

A joyful heart makes a face cheerful, but a sad heart produces a broken spirit (Prov. 15:13).

JOY CHANGES YOUR PURPOSE
Read Acts 16:27 (before the event) and 16:34 (after the event).

Before this event, what was the jailer's main concern in life?
_____
_____

After receiving Christ, the jailer saw the glory of the Lord and had great joy. What do you think his new purpose in life was?
_____

2-TRYING TO FIND JOY WON'T WORK

We know that joy will change our lives for the better, so how do we find it? Unfortunately, "trying to find joy" usually does not result in joy at all.

Have you ever been "down in the dumps"? If so, have you tried to get yourself out of the "blues"? Many people try to get rid of their emotional down times.

What ways have you tried, or have you seen people try, to get rid of depression? Check all that apply.
☐ **Buying things**
☐ **Sleeping**
☐ **Going to a movie or sporting event**
☐ **Going out to eat**
☐ **Going to church**
☐ **Working really hard at school or work**
☐ **Food, alcohol, or drugs**

All of us have tried some of these things. But will trying to have joy get you joy? Read Proverbs 14:12-13. What do these two verses tell us about trying to get joy? _____
_____
_____

The truth is, the harder you try to make yourself happy, the more likely you are to end up miserable. Here is why: If you try and it doesn't work (and it won't), you figure things are never going to be joyous; and then you are even more depressed.

When the jailer woke up and saw the doors of the prison open, he drew his sword and was going to kill himself, since he thought the prisoners had escaped (Acts 16:27).

He [the jailer] brought them up into his house, set a meal before them, and rejoiced because he had believed God with his entire household (Acts 16:34).

There is a way that seems right to a man, but its end is the way to death. Even in laughter a heart may be sad, and joy may end in grief (Prov. 14:12-13).

God's Offer of Joy

Read Ecclesiastes 2:1-9 in your Bible. What was Solomon trying to do?
☐ Get wealthy
☐ Make a name for himself
☐ Serve God
☐ Find happiness and joy

Therefore, I hated life because the work that was done under the sun was distressing to me. For everything is futile and a pursuit of the wind (Eccl. 2:17).

Solomon was trying as hard as he could to find joy. Read Ecclesiastes 2:17. What was the result?
☐ He learned a lot.
☐ He became miserable.
☐ He had some good times.
☐ He got to write about his joy.

The bottom line is that you can try to find joy; but in the end, you are better off if you never even looked for it.

3-JOY FINDS YOU

It is a strange thing to consider, but in many ways you don't find joy. It finds you.

You did not choose Me [Jesus], but I chose you. I appointed you that you should go out and produce fruit, and that your fruit should remain, so that whatever you ask the Father in My name, He will give you (John 15:16).

Read John 15:16. Who did the choosing when it came to who got to be a disciple of Jesus?
☐ The disciples chose.
☐ Jesus chose.
☐ The church chose.
☐ Circumstances chose.

This verse shows an important truth. Before we even follow Jesus, He has already chosen us. He doesn't force us to be His follower, and He doesn't overlook some people and favor others. But Jesus chooses us first, and our response is to accept what He has laid before us.

It works the same way with joy. Jesus chooses to give us joy. We don't seek after joy; we just accept what He has laid out before us.

Read John 10:10. What did Jesus choose for all His followers to have?

☐ A new car
☐ The right of passage
☐ An abundant life
☐ Four reliable friends

"A thief comes only to steal and to kill and to destroy. I have come that they may have life and have it in abundance" (John 10:10).

Jesus wants so much for you to have joy that He will even seek you out when you are sad.

Read Luke 24:13-14. What was going on here? _____
_____

Read Luke 24:15. Who joined up with these two guys?

_____

Now that same day two of them were on their way to a village called Emmaus, which was about seven miles from Jerusalem. Together they were discussing every-thing that had taken place (Luke 24:13-14).

Read Luke 24:17. What was the general mood of these two guys? _____
_____

Now get this. Two followers of Jesus were sad because of His death. Jesus sought them out. Then Jesus told them the truth about Himself and revealed Himself to them.

And while they were dis-cussing and arguing, Jesus Himself came near and began to walk along with them (Luke 24:15).

Read Luke 24:32-35 in your Bible. What happened next? _____
_____
_____
_____

You see, Jesus loved these men so much that He hunted them down on an old, dusty road to turn their hearts from sorrow to joy. He will do the same thing for you if you are willing to accept His offer.

Then He [Jesus] asked them, "What is this dispute that you're having with each other as you are walking?" And they stopped walking and looked discouraged (Luke 24:17).

4-TALK ABOUT JOY

1. How has God's joy changed your life so far?
2. Why do you think it is impossible for you to make yourself happy?
3. Why does God seek us out to give us joy?
4. What have you learned about joy thus far that changes the way you look at joy?

✦ DAY 4: ACCEPTING THE OFFER

Two miserable weeks passed after Rex walked away from God's offer of joy. But God drew him back to the same church. This time when the preacher gave the congregation the opportunity to accept God's offer of joy and happiness, Rex responded by faith. And you won't believe how everything has changed for him since that night.

1-THE OFFER

Right now, Jesus makes you an incredible offer. You can have His joy for the rest of your life! Who wouldn't want that?

Surprisingly, many people in the Bible did not want Jesus' offer of joy. Perhaps they didn't believe Jesus could really deliver joy. Perhaps they were afraid to turn loose of their own life and let Jesus totally run things.

> A ruler asked Him [Jesus], "Good Teacher, what must I do to inherit eternal life?" … "You know the commandments: Do not commit adultery; do not murder; do not steal; do not bear false witness; honor your father and mother." "I have kept all these from my youth," he said. When Jesus heard this, He told him, "You still lack one thing: sell all that you have and distribute it to the poor, and you will have treasure in heaven. Then come, follow Me." After he heard this, he became extremely sad, because he was very rich (Luke 18:18,20-23).

Read Luke 18:18,20-23. What did this guy want from Jesus?
☐ **Directions to Jerusalem**
☐ **Eternal life**
☐ **An answer to a tough question**
☐ **To be healed**

The guy was searching for eternal life. In Jesus' plan, eternal life is the joyous life; and it begins when we accept Him. Jesus never viewed eternal life as something that started with death. Eternal life starts with a relationship with Jesus.

What did Jesus offer this man? Check all that apply.
☐ **Heartache and disappointment**
☐ **Treasure in heaven**
☐ **The chance to be a follower**
☐ **Real joy**

Do you get it? Jesus offered this man the chance to have His joy. What an awesome opportunity! As we have seen, joy comes when we see and experience God's glory. Jesus was giving this man the chance to have this kind of joy.

What did the man do?_____

As the man walked away, the Bible said he was sad. Why do you think he was sad? _____

_____

He had a chance to see God's glory, but he didn't accept the offer. Why? Read verse 23. Why did he reject Jesus? _____

_____

This man rejected joy because things got in the way. These things didn't bring the man joy; they just got in the way. Think about the things that can get in your way of accepting Jesus' offer of joy.

2-THE OFFER IS WITHDRAWN

The offer of joy that will not fade is on the table right now for you! However, the offer will not always be there.

Read Luke 19:1-10 in your Bible. This story is similar to that of the rich, young ruler. This guy, Zacchaeus, had plenty of things. But he was looking for something more. His search led him up a tree. When Jesus found him, He made Zach an offer similar to the one He offered the ruler in chapter 18.

Read verse 5. What did Jesus say to Zach? Check all that apply.
☐ **Come down immediately.**
☐ **It is going to happen today.**
☐ **Take your time making up your mind.**
☐ **Have a good day.**

What do you think would have happened if Zach had decided to wait a while before accepting Jesus' offer? _____

_____

_____

_____

God offers you the chance to see and experience His glory. When that happens, you will find real joy. However the offer, which is available now, may or may not be available at some date in the future.

Read Matthew 25:6-13 in your Bible. In this story, some people missed the joy of the wedding because they weren't ready. Then when they were ready, the door was shut.

When they called out (from outside the wedding), what did the doorkeeper say to them?_____ _____

_____

What do you think that means for you?_____

_____

_____

3-RESPONDING

After four days of study, hopefully you realize that you find joy when you see and experience the glory of God. So how do you respond to that? You begin by turning your emotions over to Him. Pray this prayer: "Living God, take total control of my emotions."

The next step is to ask God to allow you to see His glory everywhere you go. Pray this prayer: "Oh Lord, I desire to see and experience Your glory wherever I am. Let me see Your glory, Lord."

As you respond to God's offer in prayer, believe that He will answer these prayers. It is God's will for you to allow Him to control your emotions. It is God's will for you to see His glory.

> "If you then, who are evil, know how to give good gifts to your children, how much more will the heavenly Father give the Holy Spirit to those who ask Him?" (Luke 11:13).

Read Luke 11:13. Here Jesus promised ...
   "the H_____ S_____ to those who a_____"

All believers have the Holy Spirit, but what Jesus was talking about here was being controlled by the Spirit. This is exactly what you are asking for when you ask for God to control your emotions and show you His glory. So ask!

4-TALK ABOUT JOY

1. Why do you have to accept Jesus's offer of joy?
2. Do you think God will ever withdraw His offer of joy? When?
3. How can you see God's glory in your everyday life?
4. How can you respond to this offer?

✴ DAY 5: WHEN THINGS GO GOOD

Kelly had just been elected student body president. She came home and threw herself on her bed and began to cry. Her mom heard her and ran into her room and asked her what was wrong. She just said, "Everything!"

What was wrong with Kelly? She was discovering that just because things go your way doesn't always mean you will be happy. Reactions like Kelly's are fairly common.

1-GOOD TIMES DO NOT EQUAL JOY

You would think that when times are good for you, you would automatically have joy. Situations such as making a good grade at school, going out with the person you like, and getting your first car should be filled with excitement and celebration.

But if that were true, how can we explain these alarming facts: (1) There are more suicides during the spring than any other time of year. (2) The birth of a baby often brings on depression for the mother. (3) Some high school seniors are depressed at graduation.

Why do the events that should bring us joy often bring the exact opposite? Read Job 31:24-28. Job was a man who, in the past (before the events in the Book of Job took place), had many good things happen to him.

What did Job warn against? Check all that apply.
- ☐ **Trusting in gold**
- ☐ **Rejoicing over wealth**
- ☐ **Being happy over accomplishments**
- ☐ **Being enticed by nature**

If I placed my confidence in gold or called fine gold my trust, if I have rejoiced because my wealth is great or because my own hand has acquired so much, if I have gazed at the sun when it was shining or at the moon moving in splendor, so that my heart was secretly enticed and I threw them a kiss, this would also be a crime deserving punishment, for I would have denied God above (Job 31:24-28).

Actually, Job warned us about all of these seemingly good things. Why? Read verse 28. Job knew looking to these good things for joy would have resulted in him having …

"d_____ G_____ a_____."

2-WHY GOOD TIMES CAN BRING BIG SORROW

There are two reasons that good times can bring about sorrow and sadness.

FIRST—UNREALISTIC EXPECTATIONS

There is a belief among Christians and non-Christians alike that if good things happen, then you will have joy, you will be happy. Solomon was a man who had all sorts of good things happen to him: money, power, women, and wisdom. You would think this guy would have joy. You would think, based on expectations, he would just be happy all the time.

All that my eyes desired, I did not deny them. I did not refuse myself any pleasure, for I took pleasure in all my struggles. This was my reward for all my struggles. When I considered all that I had accomplished and what I had labored to achieve, I found everything to be futile and a pursuit of the wind. There was nothing to be gained under the sun (Eccl. 2:10-11).

Read Ecclesiastes 2:10-11. What was Solomon's view of all the good things that happened to him? _____
_____
_____
_____

Solomon finally realized this and wrote down his conclusion about joy in Proverbs 10:28. What did he say?
☐ **You need things to have joy**
☐ **Expectations come to nothing**
☐ **There are no joyful people in church**
☐ **Looking for joy is joy itself**

Solomon discovered that when you are hoping that things or even people will give you joy, you are going to be disappointed even in the good times. Things and people won't bring lasting joy; it is unrealistic and impractical to expect good things to bring lasting joy.

The hope of the righteous is joy, but the expectation of the wicked comes to nothing (Prov. 10:28).

SECOND—THE NATURAL LETDOWN

If you are looking to good things (but not God) to bring you joy, there is a natural letdown when you get good things. This is exactly what happened with Kelly!

This happens because joy is related to emotions, and no good thing, no matter how good, can keep your emotions up. You can't keep your own emotions up either. Emotions driven to joy by good things and good times will eventually crash, and so will the joy.

A good example of this in the Bible is Elijah. In 1 Kings 18, Elijah had taken on 450 false prophets and had won. He was so pumped, so full of joy, that according to Kings 18:44-46, Elijah out-ran the chariot of Ahab from Carmel to Jezreel, a distance of 17 miles.

How would you describe a man who out-ran a chariot for 17 miles? _____
_____

Yet look what happened next. Jezebel threatened to kill Elijah.

Read 1 Kings 19:3-5. How would you describe Elijah in these verses? _____
_____
_____

How could a guy be so pumped, so fearless, so full of joy one minute and become suicidal the very next day? It's the natural letdown.

If we realize that letdowns are possible and we realize that our joy comes from seeing and experiencing the glory of God, we don't have to have a letdown. But just remember, good times without the glory of God will lead to letdowns.

3-THE KEY TO JOY IN THE GOOD TIMES

When good times come to you, and they will, there is one key to being sure you have joy through the good times. That key is to be sure and give God the glory for all the good times both publicly and privately.

Look at the strange story of King Herod in Acts 12:21-23. Herod was an enemy of God, but God never touched him until one day.

What did Herod do that brought God's wrath? _____
_____
_____

Then Elijah became afraid and immediately ran for his life. When he came to Beer-sheba that belonged to Judah, he left his servant there, but he went on a day's journey into the wilderness. He sat down under a broom tree and prayed that he might die. He said, "I have had enough! LORD, take my life, for I'm no better than my fathers." Then he lay down and slept under the broom tree (1 Kings 19:3-5).

On an appointed day, dressed in royal robes and seated on the throne, Herod delivered a public address to them. The populace began to shout, "It's the voice of a god and not of a man!" At once an angel of the Lord struck him because he did not give the glory to God, and he became infected with worms and died (Acts 12:21-23).

Herod accepted praise due to God for a good speech he had given. The result was that Herod's joy left him pretty quickly as he was …

"i_____ with w_____ and d_____."

The same is not likely to happen to you. But the only way to have joy in good times is to give the glory for the good times to God. Then, as you see God getting the glory, you get joy!

4-TALK ABOUT JOY
1. Why do good times not equal joy?
2. Have good times ever brought you sorrow? How?
3. How could Kelly have kept the joy in her election?
4. What can you do to have real joy when things go good?

1. *Blue Letter Bible.* "Dictionary and Word Search for 'simchah (Strong's 08057)'". Blue Letter Bible. 1996-2002. 25 Feb 2004. <*http://www.blueletterbible.org/cgi-bin/words.pl?word=08057&page=1*>.
2. *Theological Dictionary of the New Testament,* s.v. "joy."

CHAPTER 4

JOY DAY TO DAY

God offers you joy in His Son, Jesus. As you allow Jesus to take control of your soul, you are doing the very thing that brings people joy, namely seeing and experiencing God's glory. However, you can lose your joy if you get your focus off of Him and onto yourself. Is it possible to have joy every day? Absolutely! Jesus promised us an abundant life.

The Big Picture

This week we will look at how it is possible to have joy day to day. We will see the following:

☐ The importance of celebration.
☐ How to ensure bad times don't end your joy.
☐ How to have joy on an ongoing basis.
☐ Why giving is essential to joy.
☐ How to give joy away.

As you approach each day's study, pray for God to give you insight into joy and how He will provide it each day. Allow Him to be your teacher and allow His Word to penetrate your heart.

Scripture

This week memorize and meditate on 1 Thessalonians 5:16-18.

For your private devotional reading this week, read the following selected Psalms related to joy.
Day 1—Psalm 5
Day 2—Psalm 16
Day 3—Psalm 30
Day 4—Psalm 33
Day 5—Psalm 47
Day 6—Psalm 95
Day 7—Psalm 98

Prayer Thought

Let this thought be in your mind this week and pray this to God as you go about your day: *Father, cause me to focus on You. To see You, oh God, and not my circumstances.*

✷ DAY 1: CELEBRATE

Anna and Demico both grew up in church. They met in college and "fell in love." Not really grounded in God's way of purity, and having no desire to save sex for marriage, they "celebrated" their love by moving in together. As things would go, they ended up sharing an apartment for their last three years of college. When they graduated they decided it would then be a good idea to get married. After all, they both wanted to "celebrate" graduation by having children.

The wedding was beautiful. Anna's wedding gown was awesome. Everyone thought they were the perfect couple. Following the wedding, a reception was held at the local country club—it was time to "celebrate." Although not known as big drinkers, Anna and Demico both became drunk at the reception. It got so bad that they passed out and had to be carried to their hotel room. When they woke up the next day, they began a marriage that turned out to be anything but a celebration. The sad thing is that these two never understood what it means to celebrate.

1-CELEBRATING GOOD TIMES

OK, so good times don't equal joy. But what should you do when good times come? Celebrate!

Normally, when something good happens (like you get accepted to Harvard), you go and tell your friends about how fortunate you are. Then, to memorialize the situation, you might eat a ton of food or buy yourself a new dress or even take a trip to an amusement park. These things are not evil. But they are ways of celebrating that focus on us—our wants, our friends, our own desires. It sounds like a lot of fun, but the joy produced in this type of celebrating will soon fade. There is another way to celebrate.

Read Jeremiah 9:23-24. Here Jeremiah was warning about improper boasting, but the same principle could apply to improper celebrating. Celebration that focuses on my wisdom, my strength, and my riches is improper. That kind of celebrating exalts me.

This is what the LORD says: "The wise must not boast in his wisdom; the mighty must not boast in his might; the rich must not boast in his riches. But the one who boasts should boast in this, that he understands and knows Me—that I am the LORD, showing faithful love, justice, and righteousness on the earth, for I delight in these things." This is the LORD's declaration (Jer. 9:23-24).

> The Seventy returned with joy, saying, "Lord, even the demons submit to us in Your name." He said to them, "I watched Satan fall from heaven like a lightning flash. Look, I have given you the authority to trample on snakes and scorpions and over all the power of the enemy; nothing will ever harm you. However, don't rejoice that the spirits submit to you, but rejoice that your names are written in heaven" (Luke 10:17-20).

What should be the focus of our boasting? _____

Likewise, what should be the focus of our celebrating?
_____

Read Luke 10:17-20. The disciples were fired up from whipping on some demons. They were celebrating this big spiritual victory. But what did Jesus say?

"Don't r_____ that the s_____ submit to y_____"

Wow. Jesus told us not even to celebrate beating up demons. Why? Because He wants us to celebrate something bigger.

Look at verse 20. What is it? _____ _____
_____

Do you see what Jesus was saying? When good times come, when you are rich, or strong, or wise, when you are leading a big ministry driving out all kinds of demons and your name is up in lights, don't boast and don't celebrate these accomplishments. Why? Because that is about you! Instead, celebrate God and His glory.

Do you get it? If, when good things happen, you celebrate who God is and what God has done, then the focus is totally off of you and onto God. You are focusing on Him and experiencing Him. He gets the glory, and you will have joy.

> Let Israel celebrate its Maker; let the children of Zion rejoice in their King. Let them praise His name with dancing and make music to Him with tambourine and lyre. For the LORD takes pleasure in His people; He adorns the humble with salvation. Let the godly celebrate in triumphal glory; let them shout for joy on their beds (Ps. 149:2-5).

Read Psalm 149:2-5. Here we see people celebrating, but what are they doing to celebrate?
- ☐ **Eating lots of good food**
- ☐ **Dancing and singing to God**
- ☐ **Going to the movies**
- ☐ **Running with the bulls**

Do you see? They celebrated not by focusing on themselves, but by focusing on God in celebration.

2—LETTING THE GOOD TIMES ROLL

We've seen that good times don't bring joy. In fact, good times can mean sorrow. And when we have good times, we should celebrate God. However, there is one aspect left. Good times don't bring joy; but at the same time, God desires for our life to have many, many, many good times.

Read John 10:10. Why did Jesus come?
☐ **To bring us good times**
☐ **To test out His power**
☐ **As an obligation to God**
☐ **To set us straight about church**

"A thief comes only to steal and to kill and to destroy. I have come that they may have life and have it in abundance" (John 10:10).

Believe it or not, Jesus came to bring us good times. These are not good times that we normally think of, like getting big bucks or taking a hot date to the prom. Instead, these good times are awesome, God-focused experiences. These in themselves do not bring joy. But these experiences are reflections of God and they point us to God. We see and experience His glory, and then we have continual joy.

So what do we do to "let the good times roll"? We don't seek the good times. Instead, the key is found in Luke 12:22-31.

Read that passage in your Bible. What is the key to letting the good times roll?
☐ **Seeking God and His kingdom**
☐ **A good cable connection**
☐ **Godly friends**
☐ **Belonging to the right church**

3—THE PARTY NEVER ENDS

One of the biggest parties thrown every year in America is in New Orleans. It is called Mardi Gras. Although this celebration is totally of the world and the flesh, it does attract great media attention. Yet one of the strangest things happens at midnight on the last day of the celebration called Fat Tuesday. At exactly midnight, the party abruptly stops. That is it. On the next day, Ash Wednesday, there are no more celebrations. Isn't it just like the world to celebrate for a few days and then call it off? But for the Christian, the celebration of God's kingdom never ends.

Jesus said to them, "Can the wedding guests be sad while the groom is with them? The days will come when the groom is taken away from them, and then they will fast" (Matt. 9:15).

"I am with you always, to the end of the age" (Matt. 28:20).

Read Matthew 9:15. What important principles are taught here?
☐ You can't be sad while the groom is present.
☐ There will be a special time for fasting.
☐ You need to be fast to get ahead.
☐ Brides and grooms grow up too fast.

In one sense, time can be divided into two segments. Segment one is when the groom is present. In that segment we party. Segment two is when the groom is not present. In that segment we fast.

In reality, segment two is actually very short. It represents the three days Jesus was in the tomb. After that time, according to Matthew 28:20 …

He is w_ _____ us a_____.

Bottom line: Since Jesus is with us all the time, the party never ends. So we can have joy all the time!

4-TALKING ABOUT JOY

1. Describe specific things you could do to celebrate good times.
2. Why does God bring good things and good times into your life?
3. What can you do to "let the good times roll"?
4. When was the last time you celebrated the presence of God?

✴ DAY 2-JOY IN THE BAD TIMES

Trey was doing just fine until his mom died unexpectedly. After that, Trey just lost all joy. He still went to school, but his mind wasn't with it. The school counselor even suggested mood-altering prescription drugs as a way to cope with his difficult times. But even after taking the pills, Trey never smiled. He just moped around all the time. Trey didn't know much, but he knew that bad times, hard times, can definitely steal your joy.

1-BAD TIMES CAN STEAL JOY

In the Old Testament, there was a man who was experiencing great joy. His name was Job. But something happened in Job's life. He lost his property and then he lost his children. When this happened, Job lost his joy.

Read Job 3:1,11. What was Job's view of life? _____
_____

Obviously, Job was pretty depressed. The depression was related to the bad things that had recently happened in Job's life. But even with things as bad as they were, there was another problem in Job's life.

After this Job began to speak and cursed the day he was born. ... "Why was I not stillborn; why didn't I die as I came from the womb?" (Job 3:1,11).

Read Job 29:1-6 in your Bible. What did Job want?
- ☐ **He wanted things to be back the way they were.**
- ☐ **He wanted to get even with Satan.**
- ☐ **He wanted to be popular.**
- ☐ **He wanted to know the Bible.**

Job longed with all his being for things to go back to the way they were. Why do you think this is a problem? _____
_____
_____

When you have bad times, there is a major tendency to sit around and long for the "good old days." Yet longing for the "good old days" will rob your joy. Why? You aren't focusing on God!

Read Psalm 33:1-3. What does God command the people to do?
- ☐ **Remember the past.**
- ☐ **Sing a new song.**
- ☐ **Cast out seven demons.**
- ☐ **Form a new committee.**

God tells people to sing a new song and shout for joy.

Rejoice in the LORD, O you righteous ones; praise from the upright is beautiful. Praise the LORD with the lyre; make music to Him with a ten-stringed harp. Sing a new song to Him; play skillfully on the strings, with a joyful shout (Ps. 33:1-3).

> Consider it a great joy, my brothers, whenever you experience various trials, knowing that the testing of your faith produces endurance. But endurance must do its complete work, so that you may be mature and complete, lacking nothing (Jas. 1:2-4).

2-A NEW VIEW OF BAD TIMES

Part of the reason we lose joy in bad times is because we don't see what God is doing in the bad times. Thus, we don't see His glory. There are two important things God is doing in bad times.

FIRST: BAD TIMES FOR GOOD RESULTS

Read James 1:2-4. Why does James say to have joy in bad times?
- ☐ Bad times can't last.
- ☐ Bad times aren't really so bad.
- ☐ Everybody has troubles.
- ☐ God uses trials to mature Christians.

God is in the process of making us mature in Christ. There are things that can be accomplished only by allowing hard times to come in your life. God doesn't make bad things happen, but God uses these things to accomplish His purpose.

> We know that all things work together for the good of those who love God: those who are called according to His purpose. For those He foreknew He also predestined to be conformed to the image of His Son, so that He would be the firstborn among many brothers (Rom. 8:28-29).

Read Romans 8:28-29. What do these verses say about God's work in us through bad times? _____
_____
_____

SECOND: BAD TIMES CAN BRING GLORY TO GOD

This may be hard for you to grasp, but in the bad times, God can be glorified. Again, God doesn't cause bad things to happen; but in the bad times, He can get the glory. Why? Because when people praise God in the bad times, His fame, His renown, His power, and His glory are even more magnified.

> Though the fig tree does not bud and there is no fruit on the vines, though the olive crop fails and the fields produce no food, though there are no sheep in the pen and no cattle in the stalls, yet I will triumph in the LORD; I will rejoice in the God of my salvation! (Hab. 3:17-18).

Read Habakkuk 3:17-18. Habakkuk lived in a really bad time. But what did he do? _____
_____
_____

As he rejoiced in God, as he was joyful, God got tremendous glory.

It is only by faith, not by sight, that people can rejoice in the bad times. When people live by faith in God, they bring glory to God because they testify that God is trustworthy and faithful.

Read Hebrews 11:35-37. How would you describe these people?
- ☐ Lucky fellows
- ☐ People with hard lives
- ☐ Misunderstood people
- ☐ The dregs of society

What is amazing is that these folks who suffered bad times like we will never know, according to verse 39 were ...

"a _____ through t_____ f_____."

God approved these people through their faith. In Hebrews 11:16 we see something else.

"God is not a_____ to be called their G_____."

God was not ashamed because His people gave Him the glory in the bad times.

3-LETTING BAD TIMES LEAD TO JOY

As we have seen, there is a purpose in the bad times. When we see the purpose, we then see and experience the presence of God. Then we can know joy in the bad times. In fact, the joy which begins in bad times can be more joyful than the joy in the good times.

Read Psalm 126:5-6. What do these verses promise about those who "sow" in sorrow? _____
_____
_____
_____

We can see that when someone sows in the bad times, he will eventually have joy. Why does that happen? The key is sowing!

Sowing, in the biblical context, generally has two meanings, both of which apply in this situation. First, *sowing* means "dying." In 1 Corinthians 15:42-44, it becomes clear that Paul understood that much of the sowing was the act of a seed falling into the ground and dying. Second, *sowing* means "giving." In 2 Corinthians 9:6 it is obvious that the way a person sows is by giving "seed."

Some men were tortured, not accepting release, so that they might gain a better resurrection, and others experienced mockings and scourings, as well as bonds and imprisonment. They were stoned, they were sawed in two, they died by the sword, they wandered about in sheepskins, in goatskins, destitute, afflicted, and mistreated (Heb. 11:35-37).

All these were approved through their faith (Heb. 11:39).

They now aspire to a better land—a heavenly one. Therefore God is not ashamed to be called their God, for He has prepared a city for them (Heb. 11:16).

Those who sow in tears will reap with shouts of joy. Though one goes along weeping, carrying the bag of seed, he will surely come back with shouts of joy, carrying his sheaves (Ps. 126:5-6).

So it is with the resurrection of the dead: Sown in corruption, raised in incorruption; sown in dishonor, raised in glory; sown in weakness, raised in power; sown a natural body, raised a spiritual body. If there is a natural body, there is also a spiritual body (1 Cor. 15:42-44).

Remember this: the person who sows sparingly will also reap sparingly, and the person who sows generously will also reap generously (2 Cor. 9:6).

How do these two come together, and what does this have to do with bad times bringing joy? When bad times come, the natural tendency is to allow them to rob you of your joy. However, if you understand that you are now dead (see Rom. 6:6) and then allow God to pour Christ in you in such a way that you meet the needs of others, God's glory is demonstrated. There is joy!

4-TALK ABOUT JOY

1. Why and how do bad times steal joy?
2. How do you view bad times?
3. How can bad times lead to God gaining glory?
4. How can you let bad times lead you to joy?

 # DAY 3-LIVING IN JOY

People like the Apostle Paul used to drive me crazy. You know the type, always up, always excited, always having joy in their lives. I use to think people like that were either faking it or they were too ignorant to understand the bad that was going on all around them.

But then I began to see that these people weren't fake and they knew what was going on around them. Finally, I became curious about the possibility of living in joy. God showed me that it is not only possible, but it is what He wants for us.

1-JOY ALL THE TIME?

So far, we have discovered that joy is an emotion God desires for us to experience. We have seen that God offers joy to us and that joy is available in the good times and in the bad. But is it really possible to live in joy on a regular basis?

Well, if you are just trying to be happy, it won't work. Eventually you'll have a bad day. Bad days will turn into bad weeks, and so on. Soon you'll have no joy at all. But it doesn't have to be that way. It is possible for you to have joy all the time!

Read 1 Thessalonians 5:16. How often does Paul tell us to be joyful?
☐ When we feel happy
☐ At least once a day
☐ Whenever we go to church
☐ All the time

> Rejoice always!
> (1 Thess. 5:16).

If Paul, led by God, admonished us to be joyful all the time, he must have believed it was possible. Yet for most Christians, it never happens. Why? Most Christians do not have joy all the time because Christ is not controlling them; He isn't allowed to be the Lord of their lives. Therefore, they are not seeing the glory of God.

Read 1 Thessalonians 5:18. Why did Paul tell these people to be joyful all the time?
☐ It was a good witness to be joyful.
☐ It was good medicine to be joyful.
☐ It was God's will for them to be joyful.
☐ It was the right time to be joyful.

> Give thanks in everything, for this is God's will for you in Christ Jesus (1 Thess. 5:18).

Did you get it? It was God's will for the people to be joyful all the time. The key is the last three words in verse 18. What are they?

"in C_____ J_____"

The key to having joy all the time is to be in Christ, and then you will see and experience the glory of God. Christ is in you all the time if you are a Christian. And you are in Christ as well. (See John 14:20.) However, to be in Christ also means for Christ to be in control of your life. In other words, it is no longer you at all; it is Christ living through you. You are out of the way, you are souled out.

> "In that day you will know that I am in My Father, you are in Me, and I am in you" (John 14:20).

2-JOY IN TIME ALONE

It is one thing to say, "I want to be joyful all the time." It is another thing to allow Christ to be in control all the time. In practical terms, there are two things you can choose to do that will make it easier for Christ to be in control of your life. Doing these things will not guarantee Christ is in control (especially if you do these things in your own strength). But if you allow Christ to work through you to do these things, then they can actually result in Christ being in control. You will then see and experience the glory of God, and then you will have joy all

"Now I am coming to You, and I speak these things in the world so that they may have My joy completed in them" (John 17:13).

"Sanctify them by the truth; Your word is truth" (John 17:17).

"Whenever you pray, you must not be like the hypocrites, because they love to pray standing in the synagogues and on the street corners to be seen by people. I assure you: They've got their reward! But when you pray, go into your private room, shut your door, and pray to your Father who is in secret. And your Father who sees in secret will reward you" (Matt. 6:5-6).

the time. These things are spending time alone with God and spending time with other Christians (fellowship).

Read John 17:13. Why did Jesus say what He said to the disciples?
_____

Jesus said all these things so that the disciples would have complete joy. How did that work?

Read John 17:17. Jesus asked God to …

s_____ the disciples by the t_____, and He proclaimed that God's W_____ was truth.

To *sanctify* means to "set apart for service." What Jesus is saying is that spending time in the Word actually sets people apart to see God's glory and to be used by Him for His glory.

Prayer is also an important part of spending time alone with God.

Read Matthew 6:5-6. What did Jesus tell us to do?_____
_____

What did Jesus say the result would be? _____
_____

As you pray, allow Christ to control your prayers and pray through you. Allow yourself to be out of the way, souled out. Then you will see and experience the glory of God. You will have continual joy.

3-JOY IN FELLOWSHIP

Besides spending time alone with God, another way to allow Christ to be in control so you see His glory is to spend time in fellowship with other Christians.

I thank God, whom I serve with a clear conscience as my forefathers did, when I constantly remember you in my prayers night and day. Remembering your tears, I long to see you so that I may be filled with joy (2 Tim. 1:3-4).

Read 2 Timothy 1:3-4. How did Paul expect to be filled with joy?
_____

Paul knew that spending time with Timothy would bring him great joy. How does fellowship bring joy?

Read 2 John 4. What brought great joy to John?
☐ Seeing the sunset
☐ Finding others walking in the truth
☐ Living a long life
☐ Cinnamon buns

John had great joy seeing others walking in the truth. Why? Because when he saw others walking in the truth he was seeing the glory of God demonstrated in their lives. When we see the glory of God in others' lives, it will bring us joy!

Also, hanging out with other Christians is an act of allowing Christ to be in control of our lives.

Read Hebrews 10:24-25. What are Christians to do?
☐ Meet together
☐ Use only simple words
☐ Encourage each other
☐ Not go to Muslim churches

As a Christian, you are instructed to go and be involved in church. It is a part of allowing Christ to control you. Because when Christ controls and you are a true part of a local church, you see God working in awesome ways. He is glorified, and you have joy all the time.

4-TALK ABOUT JOY

1. Do you believe God wants you to have joy in Him all the time?
2. How does time alone with God affect your personal joy?
3. Why does God desire for us to fellowship with other believers?
4. How close are you to "walking in truth" (2 John 4)?

I was very glad to find some of your children walking in truth, in keeping with a command we have received from the Father (2 John 4).

Let us be concerned about one another in order to promote love and good works, not staying away from our meetings, as some habitually do, but encouraging each other, and all the more as you see the day drawing near (Heb. 10:24-25).

✦ DAY 4—JOY IN GIVING

Steve listened as his pastor preached a sermon on giving. As he listened two thoughts crossed his mind: (1) giving is for adults, and (2) giving has nothing to do with salvation.

Unfortunately, like most teens, Steve had not grasped the importance of giving. It is true that most of the money in a church comes from the adults. It is also true that no amount of giving can "buy" a person's way into heaven. However, giving is absolutely related to the joy we experience while on earth. Faithful giving will be used by God to bring us joy. When you understand this, it will change your whole view on giving.

1—GIVING IS OBEDIENCE

In chapters 5 and 6 we will study "Obeying by Faith," and we will discover how obedience is really Christ doing the work. But let's see how giving is a part of obeying.

Read Malachi 3:7-10 in your Bible. What does God command us to do in these verses?
☐ **Give a tithe and offerings to God.**
☐ **Count your blessings.**
☐ **Rob from Peter to pay Paul.**
☐ **Flood the gates open.**

God says to give. There are reasons He says to give, and we will look at some of these reasons. But the reasons are not important. God says to give; and as we give, we are allowing Christ to control our minds, emotions, and most importantly, our wills. When we live with that kind of faith, God gets glory. When He gets the glory, we see His glory. When we see His glory, we experience joy.

Think about it. Why would a normally sane person, having a tough time providing for his or her family, willfully give 10 percent of his or her income to the church? That person does not give expecting to receive anything monetary in return. That person definitely could use the money. Yet he or she gives the money by faith out of obedience to God.

What does a person's giving say?
☐ **It says there must be a God, or why else would he give?**
☐ **It says God must provide, or why else would she trust Him by giving up money that is needed?**
☐ **It says the church must be God's body on earth, or why else would he give to the church?**

The point is that giving is an act of obedience and guess who gets the glory for that act? God. Remember, He gets glory; you get joy.

2-GIVING CHANGES OUR FOCUS

Read Luke 18:22. In this verse, Jesus told a man to sell all his stuff, give it to the poor, and come and follow Him.

> When Jesus heard this, He told him, "You still lack one thing: sell all that you have and distribute it to the poor, and you will have treasure in heaven. Then come, follow Me" (Luke 18:22).

What did Jesus promise the man if he would give his stuff away?
☐ **Treasure in heaven**
☐ **Forty acres of good crops**
☐ **New friends among the poor**
☐ **Pain and sorrow**

Jesus wanted this guy to get his focus off of this world and onto the next world. This would be accomplished by giving things away, as long as they were given from the heart. Then the focus would be on the next world. The man would be able to see God's glory, and he would have joy all the time. This kind of living could only happen when Jesus was doing the giving through him!

However, as long as the man focused on things of this world, he would not see or experience God's glory. There would not be joy.

Read Luke 18:23. What word described the man after he refused to give? _____

> After he heard this, he became extremely sad, because he was very rich (Luke 18:23).

3-GIVING CHANGES OTHERS

When you give to God's work (at church), when you give to poor people, when you give to missions, God is able to take your gift and change others. When this happens, you see God's glory at work. You rejoice in His glory.

Paul received gifts from the church at Philippi. These gifts were used to support Paul in missionary work. Paul's work (God's work in Paul) literally changed the world.

Read Philippians 4:10. What was Paul's feeling concerning their gifts?_____

_____

Read Philippians 4:18. What did Paul say about the gifts of the Philippians? _____

_____

I rejoiced in the Lord greatly that now at last you have renewed your care for me. You were, in fact, concerned about me, but lacked the opportunity to show it (Phil. 4:10).

I have received everything in full, and I have an abundance. I am fully supplied, having received from Epaphroditus what you provided—a fragrant offering, a welcome sacrifice, pleasing to God (Phil. 4:18).

God was pleased with the gifts which were used to change the world through the life of Paul. In this, God's glory was seen, and the Philippians found great joy in giving gifts that brought glory to God.

I'll never forget an event that happened in my life almost 30 years ago. I was graduating from college and felt led to serve as a youth intern in a church some distance from my home town. The salary was going to be small, but I was excited about the adventure of trusting God to supply my needs.

There was a guy in our college group at church named David. He was a poor college student like I was. A short time before I was to leave, David, who already faithfully tithed to our church, came up to me and handed me a $20 bill. He said, "God told me to give this to you."

It wasn't the amount that was important, although $20 then would compare to about $80 today. It wasn't that I needed money, although I did need some money just for the trip to get to my new church. It was just the spirit in which it was given. I knew that God had spoken to David to encourage me. I was greatly encouraged, even changed, by that simple gift. David of course gave the glory to God. And you know when God gets the glory, we get joy!

Y-TALK ABOUT JOY

1. How has giving been related to joy in your life?
2. Why does being obedient bring joy?
3. How can just giving away our money change our focus?
4. What would you say to Steve who thought giving was just for adults?

⚹ DAY 5: JOY—WHAT THE WORLD NEEDS NOW

I met Ahmad on a university campus in Cairo, Egypt. He was studying engineering and was glad to speak to me as he was hoping to get to America one day. I asked him many questions about his life, which was so different from my own. He was a brilliant student who could speak many languages and understood things about physics I would never be able to grasp. But he lacked one thing—joy.

The sad thing about Ahmad is that I don't think he even knew what joy was all about. In his young life he had never experienced real joy, and he had never even known anyone else who had experienced real joy. His faith had taught him a great deal about works of discipline. But he knew nothing of the joy that comes from knowing Jesus.

1-A WORLD OF NEED

If there is one thing that is desperately needed right now in this world, it is joy. If everyone in the world had joy, there would be no terrorism, no murder, no robbery, no lying. If there was joy in every family, there would be no divorce, no broken homes, no child abuse. In fact, if you think about it, many problems in the world are brought on because people lack joy. Plus people are seeking joy in the wrong places. Drugs, alcohol, pornography, immoral behavior, materialism, and greed are some of the wrong places people look for joy. We can make laws telling people how to act. We can teach values in school, helping people to see how to be a productive part of society. But as long as people lack joy, the world's problems will just keep growing.

Read 1 Kings 21:1-6 in your Bible. Ahab was the king of Israel. By this time Ahab was already a very bad man. As the king, he had tremendous wealth and power.

What was Ahab doing in 1 Kings 21:4?
☐ **Enjoying being king**
☐ **Acting like a spoiled brat**
☐ **Worshiping God**
☐ **Trying to build a name for himself**

Ahab was acting like a spoiled brat. Why? He had no joy in his heart. He wanted something, and he couldn't have it.

Read 1 Kings 21:7-14 in your Bible. What did Jezebel, Ahab's wife, do to try to bring him joy?
☐ **Killed a good man**
☐ **Gave him a present**
☐ **Asked his advice**
☐ **Sang him a song**

Jezebel thought she could bring joy to the spoiled brat by killing someone else. How is this just like the way many people today try to find joy? _____
_____
_____
_____

Ahab said to Elijah, "So, you have caught me, my enemy." He replied, "I have caught you because you devoted yourself to do what is evil in the LORD's sight" (1 Kings 21:20).

Elijah was then ordered by God to go and bring a message to Ahab and Jezebel. What was God's message in verse 20?

"You d_____ yourself to do what is e_____."

Ahab sold his soul to evil to try to find joy. How do people try this today? _____
_____
_____

Why will this not work?_____

_____

If you read further in the story, you'll see the sad end of Ahab and Jezebel. (See 2 Kings 9:30–10:17.)

2-WHAT ARE YOU GIVING AWAY?

Don't go around trying to cheer people up. This is a mistake many people make. Trying to cheer people up may work short-term; but after the short-term joy wears off, people will be right back where they started.

Instead of trying to give away joy, give away Jesus. Sharing the gospel of Jesus results in people finding Him. As they find Him, they will get joy.

Read 1 Corinthians 1:22-23. What was the message Paul shared?
- ☐ Don't worry, be happy
- ☐ Christ crucified
- ☐ Cheer up folks
- ☐ Things could be worse

The Jews ask for signs and the Greeks seek wisdom, but we preach Christ crucified, a stumbling block to the Jews and foolishness to the Gentiles (1 Cor. 1:22-23).

You don't have to be a little bundle of good cheer to give joy away. All you need to do is be sure you give Christ away.

3-WHO IS DOING THE GIVING AWAY?

There is a tendency to get all fired up, go off, and try to win the world to Jesus. After all, Jesus and the joy He brings is what the world desperately needs. The only problem with this kind of thinking is that it will fail. Why? Because it is primarily about us and us doing something noble for Jesus. God is not going to get much glory out of our human efforts; because if we succeed in our own efforts, then we believe we deserve some of the glory.

Read Luke 22:33. What was Peter bound and determined to do?
- ☐ Get into heaven
- ☐ Go to prison with Jesus
- ☐ Catch some more fish
- ☐ Die with Jesus

"Lord," he told Him, "I'm ready to go with You both to prison and to death!" (Luke 22:33).

Peter was determined to do this great thing for Jesus because of his great love for Jesus. But think about it. If Peter did make this bold stand for Christ, he'd be getting a lot of glory himself.

How likely was Peter to succeed in his own power? _____

_____

Remember that you are souled out. If you try to witness on your own, you will fail. However if you allow Christ to do the witnessing through you, you will be out of the way, God will get the glory, and you'll have joy. Then people will come to faith in Christ.

"No one can come to Me unless the Father who sent Me draws him, and I will raise him up on the last day" (John 6:44).

Read John 6:44. What is needed for someone to come to Christ?
☐ **A good sermon**
☐ **Good music**
☐ **They must be drawn by God**
☐ **The right setting**

People will come to Christ only when He draws them to Himself. That is why it is essential for true conversion that Christ do the witnessing through you, as opposed to you witnessing on your own.

4—TALK ABOUT JOY
1. Why does the world need joy?
2. Why don't we just go around and cheer up people?
3. Who gives away joy?
4. What is the most important thing you've learned about "finding joy" this week?

CHAPTER 5

OBEYING BY FAITH

God desires for us to obey Him. It is not like God wants us to obey Him in order to ruin our lives. In fact, it is just the opposite. God wants us to obey Him so that we can have a close relationship with Him. Furthermore, God wants us to obey Him because He actually knows what is best for us, in the short haul and in the long haul.

MEMORY VERSE

Therefore as you have received Christ Jesus the Lord, walk in Him (Col. 2:6).

The Big Picture

This week you will look at how to allow your will to be souled out and how this makes it possible for Jesus to obey through you. You will see the following:
☐ What your will is all about.
☐ Why your will is a problem.
☐ How your will determines your actions.
☐ The battle that is going on over your will.
☐ How to obey by faith.

As you approach each day's study, pray for God to speak to you about your will. Allow Him to teach you out of His Word.

Scripture

This week memorize and meditate on Colossians 2:6.

For your private devotional reading this week, read Hebrews 11.
Day 1—Hebrews 11:1-3
Day 2—Hebrews 11:4-7
Day 3—Hebrews 11:8-16
Day 4—Hebrews 11:17-22
Day 5—Hebrews 11:23-29
Day 6—Hebrews 11:30-38
Day 7—Hebrews 11:39-40

Prayer Thought

Let this thought be in your mind this week and pray this to God as you go about your day: *Lord, take control of my will and live through me. Live through me.*

✴ DAY 1: THE WILL

Candace looked down at her watch. It was 3:00, meaning that school would soon be out, but dinner was still three hours away. As usual Candace felt hungry, but she had promised her mom she wouldn't eat between meals. The truth was she didn't really want to eat between meals. But every day when school was dismissed, Candace faced a major test of willpower. Would she eat or would she somehow manage to control herself and wait until dinner?

In her mind she knew eating between meals was not good for her increasing weight. Emotionally, she felt bad whenever she gave in, but happy when she stood strong. Yet when it came to her will, Candace seemed almost powerless. In a recent two-week stretch Candace had eaten a candy bar and drank a soft drink every afternoon after school. She looked at her watch and worried … *when the final bell rang would today be any different?*

1-WHAT IS THE WILL?

The mind is pretty easy to understand; it is the thinking part of a person. Emotions may be difficult to control, but it is easy to see that they are the feeling part of a person. But what exactly is the will of a person?

The word used in the New Testament for *will* is *thelema*. This word basically means "desire."[1] The will of a human is made up of a wide array of desires that are deeply woven into the person's soul.

In 1 Corinthians 7:37 Paul describes one of the desires that makes up the human will. What is that desire?
☐ **The desire for acceptance**
☐ **The desire for sexual relationships**
☐ **The desire to win**
☐ **The desire for lunch**

> **He who stands firm in his heart (who is under no compulsion, but has control over his own will) and has decided in his heart to keep his own virgin, will do well (1 Cor. 7:37).**

Interestingly, in this passage Paul said that a man who has control over his will has control over his natural desires for sexual relationships.

> But to all who did receive Him, He gave them the right to be children of God, to those who believe in His name, who were born, not of blood, or of the will of the flesh, or of the will of man, but of God (John 1:12-13).

Read John 1:12-13. What does John mean when he refers to the "will of the flesh"?
☐ **The natural desire for sexual relationships**
☐ **The desire to be boss of the family**
☐ **The desire for more money**
☐ **The desire for recognition**

We humans do contain a whole bundle of desires. Besides the desire for intimacy, we also desire to be in control of our own destinies, and even our world.

> Pilate decided to grant their demand and released the one they were asking for, who had been thrown into prison for rebellion and murder. But he handed Jesus over to their will (Luke 23:24-25).

Read Luke 23:24-25. What was the will of the crowd in this verse?
_____
_____
_____

The crowd desired Jesus dead. It was their will. Deep inside these people was a desire to run their own lives. This was their will. In a sense, Jesus was killed because of the free will of man. Will leads directly to actions.

2-THE WILL AND SOULED OUT
When someone is souled out, the person is out of the way so Jesus is in control. When Jesus is in control, He is in control of the will. Basically, a person who is souled out allows his or her will to be under the control of Jesus.

> "I delight to do Your will, my God; Your instruction resides within me" (Ps. 40:8).

Read Psalm 40:8. How would you describe the will of David as he wrote this particular psalm? _____
_____

All David desired was to do the will of God. Interestingly, he said:

"Your i_____ resides within m_____."

David was saying that in his soul, God and God's Word were totally in control.

In life you will face many tests, just like Candace. You can rely upon your own will, or you can move out of the way and be souled out, giving Jesus the opportunity to make your will His will.

When we do that, we can repeat the words of Psalm 73:25 and say …

"I d_____ nothing on e_____ but Y_____."

Whom do I have in heaven but You? And I desire nothing on earth but You (Ps. 73:25).

3-GOD'S DESIRE FOR YOUR WILL

God desires to replace your will with His will. Then your actions will actually be His actions. But what will that look like? When the Spirit is in control of your will, what will you do? In Galatians 5:22-23 we see the different aspects of the fruit of the Spirit. God desires for us to be at peace mentally and to be joyful emotionally. When it comes to the will and the way we act, God desires for the other characteristics to be reflected through the will into actions.

The fruit of the Spirit is love, joy, peace, patience, kindness, goodness, faith, gentleness, self-control (Gal. 5:22-23).

What are these other characteristics according to Galatians 5:22-23?

l_____, p_____, k_____, g_____,
f_____, g_____, and s_____

It looks very much like the diagram on page 90.

In some ways these other characteristics—love, patience, kindness, goodness, faith, gentleness, and self-control—are all acts of obedience. God has a standard, a way He desires for us to act. When He controls our wills, He controls our desires; and we will act the way He desires. This is both obedience and the evidence of the fruit of the Spirit.

Read Luke 22:42. What did Jesus pray for in the garden? Check all that apply.
☐ **The cup to be taken away**
☐ **Angels to defeat Satan**
☐ **God's will**
☐ **The second coming**

"Father, if You are willing, take this cup away from Me—nevertheless, not My will, but Yours, be done" (Luke 22:42).

Obeying by Faith

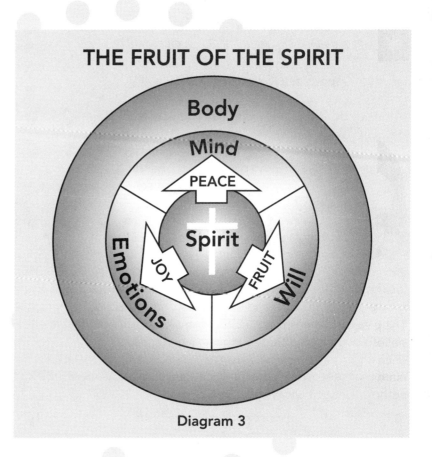

THE FRUIT OF THE SPIRIT

Body

Mind

PEACE

Spirit

JOY

FRUIT

Emotions

Will

Diagram 3

Jesus expressed two things in prayer: the immediate desire for the cup (death) to be taken away, and the ultimate desire to do only God's will. In expressing these two conflicting desires, Jesus showed us that when we are controlled by Him, all our desire—our own will—must give way to His will. There is no compromise; there is only obedience.

When God controls the will, we see things like patience, faithfulness, and self-control being shown in Jesus' obedience even unto death.

4-TALK ABOUT OBEYING

1. Why do you think Candace had such a rough time every afternoon?
2. What does it mean to you that "the will is souled out"?
3. What is God's will for your will?
4. How do you act when He is controlling you?

✴ DAY 2: THE PROBLEMS WITH THE HUMAN WILL

Jan ran on her desires. When her desires told her to date Sean, even though her parents warned against it, Jan went ahead. When her desires told her to give up her college scholarship to drop out and try her hand at painting, she went with her desires. When her desires told her it was time to end her three-year marriage to Sean, she went ahead and got a divorce. And when her desires told her to join the Army, she went with that too.

The problem was, once she got in the Army her drill sergeant didn't believe in living by desires at all. He believed in things like obedience. I'm sure you can see the difficulty of Jan's situation. She was learning that human desire and obedience to the commands of your authorities don't always go hand in hand.

1-PROBLEM ONE: HUMAN WILL IS TAINTED

We are made up of a whole bundle of desires, some of which we might even call instincts. What is wrong with that? After all, when we let our desires (our human will) run our lives, aren't we just being human? What could be wrong with being human? Plenty!

When we were created, our will was basically up for grabs. Our will could be a desire for God and godly things or a desire for us, and thus, ungodly things.

Read Genesis 2:25. Why do you think Adam and Eve, though naked, felt no shame?
☐ They were innocent.
☐ It was too early in the morning.
☐ They were young.
☐ They were confused.

Both the man and his wife were naked, yet felt no shame (Gen. 2:25).

At this point in their lives these first humans had only one desire, one will—to know God. However, that changed when their desire for God was wiped out by sin. (See Gen. 3:1-7.)

He said to the woman: "I will intensify your labor pains; you will bear children in anguish. Your desire will be for your husband, yet he will dominate you" (Gen. 3:16).

Part of God's judgment on sin is found in Genesis 3:16. What did He say to Eve?

"Your d_____ will be for your h_____."

Man's will, man's desire, which originally was only for God, became focused on other things. God even changed Adam's focus when He said in Genesis 3:19 …

"You will eat b_____ by the s_____ of your brow."

This showed how man would focus on his job and providing for his family.

"You will eat bread by the sweat of your brow until you return to the ground, since you were taken from it. For you are dust, and you will return to dust" (Gen. 3:19).

2-PROBLEM TWO: HUMAN WILL LEADS US AWAY FROM GOD

This will, totally focused on ourselves, is what has produced such a messed-up world today. Read Romans 1:21-25 in your Bible. What did God do to humans that allowed the world to be so messed up?
☐ **He made them evil.**
☐ **He gave them over to their desires.**
☐ **He caused many to hate good.**
☐ **He withdrew from their presence.**

All that God had to do was give men over to their own wills and men would worship the creation, not the Creator. Why? Our wills are tainted by sin.

3-PROBLEM THREE: HUMAN WILL RELIES ON THE FLESH

Just as with your mind and emotions, you will be controlled either from within—by the Spirit, or from without—by the flesh.

Although God would like for your will to be controlled by the Spirit, the natural tendency is for your will to be controlled by the flesh.

What does John 6:63 say about the work of the Spirit and flesh? Check all that apply.
☐ **The flesh doesn't last long.**
☐ **The Spirit gives life.**
☐ **The Spirit is given in secret.**
☐ **The flesh doesn't help at all.**

> "The Spirit is the One who gives life. The flesh doesn't help at all. The words that I [Jesus] have spoken to you are spirit and are life" (John 6:63).

The flesh is of no value, but it sure can get in the way and end up controlling our desires, our will.

Read Jude 17-19. How did Jude describe these people who lived by the flesh in verse 18?

"w_____ according to their own ungodly d_____"

What was the root of these ungodly desires (v. 19)? _____
_____

> But you, dear friends, remember the words foretold by the apostles of our Lord Jesus Christ; they told you, "In the end time there will be scoffers walking according to their own ungodly desires." These people create divisions and are merely natural, not having the Spirit (Jude 17-19).

Do you see? These folks didn't have the Spirit. They were full of human desire, ungodly desire, because they were natural people. Natural people are people after the flesh, people of this natural world.

4-TALK ABOUT OBEDIENCE
1. Why are human instincts dangerous?
2. What does it mean to you that your human will is tainted by sin?
3. When was a time recently that your will was contrary to God's will?
4. When do you find your will relying on the flesh?

✳ DAY 3: HOW WILL LEADS TO ACTIONS

Andrew couldn't believe it. His mom had given him her credit card and asked him to buy his own birthday present, with a $50 limit. Although he felt it wasn't very thoughtful of his mom not to pick out a present, Andrew figured he could get something he really wanted. But what he couldn't believe was what he actually bought. How was he going to explain to his mom that he had installed a $500 sound system in his car using her credit card?

What was he thinking? The truth is Andrew wasn't thinking; he just let his desire rule the day. Although we shake our heads at Andrew's situation, we have all had times when we let our desires dictate our actions.

1-WILL AND BEHAVIOR

It is one of the sad facts of human existence that will, not intellect or even emotion, determines our behavior. For example, intellectually we know that eating tons of pizza is bad for our health since the extra carbs will not be burned up in our normal activities. Intellectually we believe and emotionally we feel that it would be a good thing not to eat tons of pizza. Then we pick up the phone and call pizza delivery. Why? We act based on will. Our desire in this case was to eat tons of pizza, not a healthy salad.

No one undergoing a trial should say, "I am being tempted by God." For God is not tempted by evil, and He Himself doesn't tempt anyone. But each person is tempted when he is drawn away and enticed by his own evil desires. Then after desire has conceived, it gives birth to sin, and when sin is fully grown, it gives birth to death (Jas. 1:13-15).

James knew this all too well. Read James 1:13-15. What did James say about sin and desire (will)?
☐ **God doesn't tempt people to sin.**
☐ **People sin when their own desires drag them away.**
☐ **Desire actually gives birth to sin.**
☐ **We need to be better people.**

Human action is a product of human will. Read Romans 1:32. What did these people know in their minds?

☐ The history of the world.
☐ People will be people.
☐ People doing these actions deserve death.
☐ God is not afraid.

Knowing in their minds that their actions would result in death, how did these people respond? _____

_____

Why would people be so dumb as to continue doing something that they know will cause their deaths and eventual separation from God? Because their wills, not their intellect, determined their actions.

2—THE FAILURE OF WILLPOWER

You might be able to guess where we are going with this discussion. (1) Your will is basically your desire. (2) Your will is tainted by sin. You no longer desire God; you desire what the Bible calls the "lust of the flesh." (3) Your will determines your actions. So what chance have you got (we are talking about the natural man or just the ordinary human being) of doing the right thing?

The Bible is pretty clear on what chance you have. Read Romans 3:10-11. According to this, what chance do you think you have of doing the right thing (in your own power)?_____

_____

_____

Because of who you are outside of Christ—a natural man with a natural will, desiring sin—you cannot summon up willpower to stop sinning.

This truth is evident in ordinary life. Let's say you have a habit, like gossiping, which you know in your mind is wrong. You determine you are going to stop. You make vows to stop. You write notes to yourself reminding you to stop. You go to the front during an invitation and tell God you are going to stop, even asking for His help to give you the willpower to stop. Then the next day, you gossip. What went wrong?

Although they know full well God's just sentence—that those who practice such things deserve to die—they not only do them, but even applaud others who practice them (Rom. 1:32).

As it is written: "There is no one righteous, not even one; there is no one who understands, there is no one who seeks God" (Rom. 3:10-11).

The human will is tainted. You don't need to try harder to have more willpower, because when you try harder and fail again, you begin to believe that gossiping must be OK. After all, you've tried to stop with all your will and you can't stop.

> I know that nothing good lives in me, that is, in my flesh. For the desire to do what is good is with me, but there is no ability to do it (Rom. 7:18).

Even when we have a little desire, maybe a desire from God to stop, we can't do it. Read Romans 7:18. What was Paul's conclusion about doing right?
☐ I have no ability to do it.
☐ Sin is irrelevant.
☐ I can't do right.
☐ I just don't have the ability to do right.

3-THE HEAD SINNER

So far this week, we have been painting a pretty bleak picture of your will. There is a reason for that. We want you to have a pretty bleak picture of your will! It is essential that you reach a point where you come to believe that you cannot now, nor will you ever be able to live even one day in your own power without committing horrible sins.

> This saying is trustworthy and deserving of full acceptance: "Christ Jesus came into the world to save sinners"—and I am the worst of them (1 Tim. 1:15).

Read 1 Timothy 1:15. How did Paul compare himself (in the flesh) to the notorious sinners of his day?
☐ He saw them as despicable.
☐ Paul saw himself as the worst sinner of them all.
☐ Paul knew he was a pretty good guy.
☐ Paul didn't like sinners.

Paul believed in his mind that in the flesh he was the worst sinner on the face of the earth. He was totally defeated by his lack of willpower. This is why he said in Romans 7:18 …

"Nothing good lives in m_____, that is, in my f_____."

Do you feel that kind of defeat? Who do you consider worse—yourself (in your flesh) or that bully at school? _____

Who do you consider worse—yourself (in your flesh) or that drug dealer?_____

Who do you consider worse—yourself (in your flesh) or that runaway father? _____

When you finally get to this stage of defeat, when you actually discover you cannot control your actions, when you realize that you are the chief among sinners—then you are ready to obey by faith.

4-TALK ABOUT OBEDIENCE

1. How would you describe your will?
2. What determines what you will do?
3. How much willpower do you have?
4. Who is the worst sinner you know at your school?

☀ DAY 4-THE BATTLE FOR THE WILL

Jesus in the garden of Gethsemane, Paul as he wrote Romans 7, Adam and Eve in Eden. What is the common thread? They all were facing a battle of wills. It is a battle that goes on daily in your life. Only, if you are like most, you lose way too many of these battles. But there is a way out. There is a way of victory.

1-THE BATTLE IS ON

Your old will, a part of your soul, is flawed and tainted by sin. Even when you desire to do right (and that isn't all the time, is it?), you can't do right. Read Romans 7:18 again. Paul summed it up pretty well when he said …

> **"For the desire to do what is g_____ is with me, but there is no a_____ to do it."**

Why could he not carry it out? His willpower was not strong enough to overcome the sinful desires that actually had control of his will.

I do not understand what I am doing, because I do not practice what I want to do, but I do what I hate (Rom. 7:15).

According to Romans 7:15, what did Paul do? Check all that apply.
☐ **The very thing he didn't want to do**
☐ **What he hated**
☐ **What Jesus did**
☐ **What he wanted to do**

There was a very real battle going on in the life of Paul. On one side of the battle was the new Paul, now a new creature in Christ. This new man had a God-given desire to love God and serve God. On the other side of the battle was the flesh-based will. The old Paul was actually dead, no longer in the picture; but since Paul lived in a body of flesh, the old desires, the old will, was still active.

What a wretched man I am! Who will rescue me from this body of death? (Rom. 7:24).

This conflict between the human will and God's will was driving Paul crazy. In Romans 7:24 Paul even said he was …

"a w_____ m_____."

Why would he call himself a wretched man? Because this battle was eating him up. Paul even cried out (v. 24), …

"Who will r_____ m_____ from this body of d_____?"

What about you? Do you sense a battle going on in your body between your human will and God's will?_____
_____
_____
_____
_____
_____

2-THE STANDARD

There is a tendency to see the battle that is raging and just join right in. We begin to approach life with a "What Would Jesus Do?" attitude. We force ourselves to become more disciplined. We acquire accountability partners and join accountability groups. We are in a battle, and we are determined that God will win out in our lives. There is only one problem—the standard.

Read James 2:10. What does this verse tell us about God's standard for righteous living?
- [ ] God is happy when we give it our best shot.
- [ ] If you "blow it" just once, you're guilty of every sin in the book.
- [ ] Keep trying even if you mess up.
- [ ] God is not concerned about your sin.

> For whoever keeps the entire law, yet fails in one point, is guilty of breaking it all (Jas. 2:10).

God has set a standard, and it is perfection. What did Jesus tell His followers in Matthew 5:48?

"Be p_____, therefore, as your heavenly F_____ is p_____."

> "Be perfect, therefore, as your heavenly Father is perfect" (Matt. 5:48).

How can you do this? You already know your will is tainted. You already know there is a battle going on inside of you between God's will and your own tainted will. Now you know that if you let your will control your life one time, you lose the battle.

What you don't realize is that the standard of perfection is actually there to drive you to the only hope—Jesus.

In the Old Testament the standard of perfection was called "the law." The law is the many commands of God that He set before men and said in effect, "Live like this." But what was the purpose of the law of perfection? What was the purpose of this standard?

Read Galatians 3:24. What was the purpose of the law?
- [ ] To show us how to live
- [ ] To lead us to live by faith in Christ
- [ ] To make us miserable
- [ ] To make us good Christians

> The law, then, was our guardian until Christ, so that all could be justified by faith (Gal. 3:24).

The law, God's holy standard, was given to show us how to live in relation to God. The problem, of course, is that none of us can live up to that standard! But in showing us our sinfulness and inability to be righteous on our own, it also points us to Christ. It leads us to a life that is based on faith in Christ and Christ alone. You see, only when we realize that we can't live this perfect life do we turn to another way. That way is Jesus.

3-A TALE OF TWO TREES

You might be wondering how this battle began and why you are doomed to fight a battle you can't win. This battle is as old as creation itself.

> The LORD God caused to grow out of the ground every tree pleasing in appearance and good for food, including the tree of life in the midst of the garden, as well as the tree of the knowledge of good and evil (Gen. 2:9).

Read Genesis 2:9. What were the two most significant trees in Eden? _____

_____

_____

The tree of life represents Jesus, the "Planter" of the tree. There is no doubt that He is the tree of life.

> Jesus told him, "I am the way, the truth, and the life. No one comes to the Father except through me" (John 14:6).

What did He say about himself in John 14:6?

"I am the way, and the truth, and the l_____."

Furthermore, in Revelation 22:14 we see that having the tree of life is required for entrance into heaven.

> "Blessed are those who wash their robes, so that they may have the right to the tree of life and may enter the city by the gates" (Rev. 22:14).

The tree of the knowledge of good and evil represents many things: the law, works, morality, and so forth. But of all the things it represents, perhaps the most deadly is simply human will. Adam and Eve didn't pick the fruit of that tree based on an intelligent decision. They knew if they picked it they would die. They didn't pick it based on emotions. They didn't have a strong emotional feeling for the tree. They picked it by will, by human will. (See Gen. 3:6.)

Eve looked at the tree and it was d_____.

Human desire, human will, picked the fruit from that tree. The result was death for all people, because human will, human desire, made the wrong choice.

> What a wretched man I am! Who will rescue me from this body of death? I thank God through Jesus Christ our Lord! So then, with my mind I myself am a slave to the law of God, but with my flesh, to the law of sin (Rom. 7:24-25).

What did Paul say (in Rom. 7:24-25) was his only hope of escaping the hold human will, a body of death, had on him?
- ☐ A fired-up church
- ☐ Good parents
- ☐ Fewer fights
- ☐ Jesus

Jesus has won the battle of wills. When He said "not My will, but Yours" (Luke 22:42), He reversed the decision made by Adam and Eve. Now as you allow Christ to live in you by faith, you are able to pick the tree of life. Tomorrow we will focus on how to obey by faith.

4-TALK ABOUT OBEDIENCE

1. Do you see a battle going on in your life?
2. What is the standard God holds up?
3. Why did God make perfection the standard?
4. How can Jesus win this battle for you?

✴ DAY 5-TO OBEY BY FAITH

 Cindy has always had a hard time doing what Jesus would do. She tried to be a good Christian, but it seemed to her that the harder she tried the more she failed. In her desperate search for an answer to her failings, she tried every self-help book that came along. Books like *Ten Ways to Stop Lying* and *How to Become an Awesome Church Member* were scattered all over her room.

When the books didn't help, she turned to conferences and retreats. She attended one retreat after another. She had a shelf full of conference notebooks loaded down with notes from the latest gurus. Whatever anyone said she would try, but still nothing worked. Finally Cindy's mom recommended she try to live the Christian life the same way she began the Christian life—by faith. Cindy had been all around it, but she had never heard that simple truth.

1-HOPE

The only hope in our battle is to obey by faith. The standard of perfection shows us that it is hopeless to try and obey by human will. The tale of two trees demonstrates how humans have failed from the beginning. But obeying by faith is totally different than anything you have ever tried before.

Test yourselves to see if you are in the faith. Examine yourselves. Or do you not recognize for yourselves that Jesus Christ is in you? (2 Cor. 13:5).

Therefore as you have received Christ Jesus the Lord, walk in Him (Col. 2:6).

So just what is obeying by faith? It is actually a combination of two simple truths found in 2 Corinthians 13:5 and Colossians 2:6.

"Do you not recognize for yourselves that J_____ C_____ is in y_____?"

"As you have received C_____ Jesus the L_____, w_____ in Him."

Together, these two verses explain what obeying by faith is all about. Obeying by faith is believing that Christ is in you and allowing Him to live out obedience to His Father through you.

2-BELIEVING CHRIST IS IN YOU

Let's be honest. Most Christians don't think about Christ being in them. They don't understand the significance. They hear people talk about it, but they don't believe it. Why? Two reasons. First, they don't feel like He is inside of them. Second, they don't see Him doing anything in them. What they fail to realize is that feeling Him and seeing Him do something only happens after they believe He is in there.

This is because God desires for us to live by faith. Living by faith means first we believe, then we feel, then we see. God wants us to live by faith because while on earth, faith is the only way we can develop a relationship with Him. That is His real goal, not just to be in us, but to have a relationship with us.

This is according to the purpose of the ages, which He made in the Messiah, Jesus our Lord, in whom we have boldness, access, and confidence through faith in Him (Eph. 3:11-12).

Read Ephesians 3:11-12. How do we approach God to develop a relationship?
☐ **By being good**
☐ **By confessing sin**
☐ **By going to church**
☐ **By faith in Him**

How can you really know Jesus is inside of you?_____
_____
_____
_____
_____
_____

You know by faith in what the Bible actually says and by faith in Jesus' promise.

What is Jesus' promise in Revelation 3:20? _____
_____
_____
_____
_____

"Listen! I stand at the door and knock. If anyone hears My voice and opens the door, I will come in to him and have dinner with him, and he with Me" (Rev. 3:20).

What does John 14:17 say about the Holy Spirit?
☐ He is coming to all good Christians.
☐ We know Him.
☐ He will be in us.
☐ The world doesn't know the Spirit.

"He is the Spirit of truth, whom the world is unable to receive because it doesn't see Him or know Him. But you do know Him, because He remains with you and will be in you" (John 14:17).

Right now, do you believe He is in you? _____

3-ALLOWING HIM TO LIVE OUT OBEDIENCE TO HIS FATHER THROUGH YOU

Next week we will explore this in detail. But think of it this way. Once you realize that He is in you, it is a matter of His will or your will. That is where the choice comes into the picture. By faith you must choose to let Him live His will, His desires, through you. It must be a faith choice because if you allow your will to have any say in the matter, your will is going to choose from human desire.

Even someone as committed as Paul recognized that he had to make a faith choice to allow Christ to live His will through him. While in prison, probably facing execution, Paul expressed his personal choice for his future.

I am pressured by both. I have the desire to depart and be with Christ—which is far better—but to remain in the flesh is more necessary for you. Since I am persuaded of this, I know that I will remain and continue with all of you for your advancement and joy in the faith (Phil. 1:23-25).

What was that choice in Philippians 1:23? _____
_____

Even though his will was to be with Christ (a godly choice), Paul made a faith choice. What did he choose by faith in verses 24-25?
_____
_____

Here it is important to see that all Paul chose was to allow God to have His way. If it meant living on, he was fine with that. That was God's decision, not Paul's.

To let Jesus live through you, go to Him in prayer all the time and say "Live through me, Jesus, live through me." Allowing Him to do that all the time is a faith choice that is made over and over again during the day.

4-TALK ABOUT OBEDIENCE

1. Why is obeying by faith your only hope of doing the right thing?
2. When you obey by faith, what happens to your will?
3. Do you believe Christ is living in you right now? If yes, why?
4. Explain in your words what you think obeying by faith is.

1. *Blue Letter Bible.* "Dictionary and Word Search for 'thelema (Strong's 2307)'". Blue Letter Bible. 1996-2002. 2 Mar 2004. *<http://www.blueletterbible.org/cgi-bin/words.pl?word=2307&page=1>.*

CHAPTER 6

KEEPING IN STEP

Clearly God desires for all people to obey Him. For the Christian, obedience is a good thing as it leads to love, patience, kindness, goodness, faithfulness, gentleness, and self-control. Yet many Christians do not regularly display the fruit of the Spirit. This fruit is produced when the Spirit is in control of one's life. But how do you allow Him to control your will all the time? The answer lies in exchanging your life for His, and then becoming internally aware of the leading of the Spirit. That is what obeying by faith is all about.

MEMORY VERSE

If we live by the Spirit, we must also follow the Spirit (Gal. 5:25).

The Big Picture

This week you will look at how someone can keep in step with the Spirit on a minute-by-minute basis. You will see the following:
☐ What it means to exchange your life for His.
☐ How to become internally aware that He is living through you.
☐ How to tell when you are out of step by His voice and His Word.
☐ The roles prayer and people play in keeping us in step.
☐ How to move beyond commitments to faith.

Scripture

This week memorize and meditate on Galatians 5:25.

For your private devotional reading this week, read the following selected passages from Galatians.
Day 1—Galatians 1:11-24
Day 2—Galatians 2:15-21
Day 3—Galatians 3:6-14
Day 4—Galatians 3:19-29
Day 5—Galatians 5:1-6
Day 6—Galatians 5:16-26
Day 7—Galatians 6:12-16

Prayer Thought

Let this thought be in your mind this week and pray this as you go about your day: *Almighty God, You live in me. Take my will and let it be only Your will. Only Your will, Jesus.*

✴ DAY 1: THE GREAT EXCHANGE

When Ashley Kelley graduated from college in the late nineties, she felt God calling her to Africa to serve as a missionary. In a short time she was appointed a journeyman missionary by the International Mission Board.

Following her term in Botswana, Africa, she returned to America. Soon, however, she felt God calling her to Canada and was appointed a missionary to Canada by the North American Mission Board. After arriving in Ottawa, Canada, she felt led by God to be involved in the launch of a new church.

Recently I talked with her and I commented that it must be difficult working in places so far from home in such tough climates. She replied, "It would be difficult if I were the one actually doing it."

Ashley had discovered what it means to obey by faith. Last week you learned that obeying by faith means believing that Christ is in you and allowing Him to live out obedience to His Father through you. To do that, first you must understand a principle of faith. He isn't just in your life. He is your life.

Read one of the key verses in all of the Bible, Galatians 2:20. What does this verse say about your relationship with Christ?

_____

_____

This verse expresses the two great exchanges of the Christian life.

1-THE FIRST EXCHANGE: I DIED WITH CHRIST

What does Romans 6:6 say happened to us?
☐ We were crucified with Christ.
☐ Jesus died alone.
☐ We need to die to self.
☐ Life begins with pain.

> I have been crucified with Christ, and I no longer live, but Christ lives in me. The life I now live in the flesh, I live by faith in the Son of God, who loved me and gave Himself for me (Gal. 2:20).

> We know that our old self was crucified with Him in order that sin's dominion over the body may be abolished, so that we may no longer be enslaved to sin (Rom. 6:6).

> **Therefore, my brothers, you also were put to death in relation to the law through the crucified body of the Messiah, so that you may belong to another—to Him who was raised from the dead—that we may bear fruit for God (Rom. 7:4).**

The Bible says that when Jesus died on the cross, your old self was right there with Him. In fact, Romans 7:4 says …

> "You also were put to d_____ in relation to the law through the c_____ body of the M_____."

This means that your old self was present in Jesus on the cross. This can only become real in your life by faith. You must accept and believe it for only one reason—God said it.

2-THE SECOND EXCHANGE: HE NOW LIVES IN ME

Once you believe that you died on the cross, you really can't explain your existence, can you? After all, how can a dead person live? The only way to explain your existence is to believe someone else is alive inside of you.

> **Therefore, we are ambassadors for Christ; certain that God is appealing through us, we plead on Christ's behalf, "Be reconciled to God" (2 Cor. 5:20).**

Read 2 Corinthians 5:20, then fill in the blanks.

> "Therefore, we are a_____ for Christ; certain that God is a_____ through us."

Do you get it? He is living through you, making Himself known to the world through you. When you witness and reach out, it isn't you doing it; it is Him doing it through you. That is what Paul knew when he said in Romans 8:11 …

> **If the Spirit of Him who raised Jesus from the dead lives in you, then He who raised Christ from the dead will also bring your mortal bodies to life through His Spirit who lives in you (Rom. 8:11).**

> "If the S_____ … l_____ in you, then He … will also bring your m_____ b_____ to l_____ through His Spirit who l_____ in you."

As a Christian, the Holy Spirit lives in you.

3-HOW TO TURN IT OVER

In chapters 1 and 2 you learned that the three steps—surrender, renewal, and warfare—were key to your mind being controlled by the Spirit. The key to allowing Him to live through you in obedience is the same!

STEP ONE: SURRENDER

The first thing to do is surrender your will to Him. Do this by saying, "Jesus, I give up. I'm not going to try anymore to do that right thing on my own. Here, it's yours, take it."

A great example of surrender is found in the life of David. In Psalm 51:17 David wrote what God is looking for. What is it?
- ☐ **Our sacrifices**
- ☐ **Faithful attendance**
- ☐ **An explanation of our sins**
- ☐ **A broken spirit, a broken heart**

The sacrifice pleasing to God is a broken spirit. God, You will not despise a broken and humbled heart (Ps. 51:17).

In surrendering, we are confessing sin, admitting our inability, and calling out to God.

In practical terms, in order to allow Him to live through us, we must surrender on a daily basis. This is what Jesus was getting at in Luke 9:23 when He said that if anyone wanted to come after Him, he must …

Then He [Jesus] said to them all, "If anyone wants to come with Me, he must deny himself, take up his cross daily, and follow Me" (Luke 9:23).

"Take up his cross d_____."

STEP TWO: RENEWAL

We must begin our day by saying in prayer, "Jesus, I can't, but You can. You run this thing I call my life."

As the day goes on, however, your will can reenter the picture. At that time you need to renew what you did at the start of the day. Say, "Jesus, I believe that You are in me, but it appears that my will is now controlling things. So by faith, I turn it back to You."

This renewing was what Paul was talking about in 2 Corinthians 4:16 when he said …

Therefore we do not give up; even though our outer person is being destroyed, our inner person is being renewed day by day (2 Cor. 4:16).

"Our inner p_____ is being r_____ day by day."

"Day by day" here means all the time. We are renewed. We are brought back to our state of surrender all the time.

STEP THREE: WARFARE

Surrender and renewal are two simple steps. We process these by faith on a daily basis. But there is still a war going on in this universe between God and Satan. Satan tricked Adam and Eve at Eden and got them to pick the wrong tree, and he continues to find ways to get to us. Even when we are surrendering daily and renewing that on a minute-by-minute basis, we are still in a war and still face the possibility of outside attack.

In times like that we need to rely upon the armor of God found in Ephesians 6:10-18. What do you think this armor has to do with fighting against Satan? _____

_____

_____

Of key importance in repelling Satan's attacks is the shield of faith. In spiritual war, faith shields us from Satan's attacks. Here is how it works.

When you are attacked, you at once, by faith, go straight to God. Ephesians 6:18 says you ...

> "P_____ at all times in the S_____."

This means you allow the Spirit that lives in you to actually pray through you.

With every prayer and request, pray at all times in the Spirit, and stay alert in this, with all perseverance and intercession for all the saints (Eph. 6:18).

4-TALK ABOUT OBEDIENCE

1. Why was Ashley Kelley able to adapt to different situations and environments?
2. What does it mean to you that you died on the cross?
3. Explain how Christ now lives in you.
4. How can you allow Him to control you daily?

DAY 2: INTERNAL AWARENESS

Preston really wanted to live for God. He wanted it so much that he bought one of those WWJD bracelets and began to wear it. He approached each day saying, "Today I am going to do what Jesus would do!" And then off he would go to another day of failure and disappointment.

What was wrong? Preston wanted to live for Jesus, and he even had the bracelet; yet every day he blew it.

Preston's problem was that his life happened too fast for him to think through each and every situation. When a kid cut in front of him in the lunch line he didn't have time to think of a "Jesus" solution to the problem, he just reacted. And just like all of us at times, he reacted by yelling at the kid cutting in line.

Is there an answer? Maybe a new bracelet or even a WWJD tattoo? The real answer is found in internal awareness. It is possible to learn how to be internally aware—to live unafraid hearing only Jesus' voice and keeping in step with His Spirit.

1-HOW TO KEEP IN STEP
To obey by faith, you must be totally aware of when you are and when you aren't allowing Him to live through you. Only when you are aware of what is going on inside you can you renew your surrender on a regular, moment-by-moment basis.

Read Galatians 5:25. Paul said …

"If we l_____ by the S_____, we must also f_____ the Spirit."

What do you think it means to "follow the Spirit"? _____
_____
_____

If we live by the Spirit, we must also follow the Spirit (Gal. 5:25).

The Greek word translated *follow* is *stoicheo,* which means "to proceed in a row as the march of a soldier."[1] In other words, to follow the Spirit means to keep in step with the Spirit. Keeping in step with the Spirit is like keeping in step in the army. When you are in the army, you are in a platoon; and you march as one. You don't think about it; you just do it. But if you get out of step with the platoon, you immediately, instinctively realize you are out of step.

In the same way you are to be so aware of your life that when you get out of step with the Spirit, and He is no longer running your life, you know it at once and begin the process of renewal. Later you will learn how to be aware of being out of step. But for now realize that keeping in step can become an instinct thing that you do without even knowing you are doing it.

2-HOW TO HEAR ONE VOICE

Elijah was a man used by God in mighty ways, yet life happened too quickly for Elijah. In fear he ran to a mountain called Horeb. There God spoke to Elijah.

Read 1 Kings 19:8-18 in your Bible. How did God speak to Elijah?
☐ **In the wind**
☐ **In an earthquake**
☐ **In a soft voice**
☐ **In the thunder**

God's voice can be loud; but often it is a soft voice, almost like a whisper as it vibrates through your mind, emotions, and will.

"The sheep hear his [the shepherd's] voice. He calls his own sheep by name and leads them out. When he has brought all his own outside, he goes ahead of them. The sheep follow him because they recognize his voice" (John 10:3-4).

Read John 10:3b-4, then fill in the blanks.

> "The s_____ hear his v_____. ... The s_____ follow him because they r_____ his v_____."

In order to keep in step, you must recognize Jesus' voice as He speaks to you. There are many other voices that speak to you, most noticeably Satan and the flesh. Yet the Bible promises you will know and recognize Jesus' voice. Tomorrow you will explore three keys to distinguishing between the voice of God and these other voices.

3-HOW TO LIVE UNAFRAID

Many times people are close to letting Jesus run their lives, but they become afraid. They fear that He might send them to Canada where it is cold or Africa where it is hot!

God tells us time and again not to be afraid. Read Matthew 1:20. What did the angel say to Joseph? _____

_____

_____

Read Luke 1:13. What did the angel say to Zechariah? _____

_____

_____

_____

Read Luke 2:10. What did the angel say to the shepherds?

_____

_____

Read 1 John 4:18. Why doesn't God want us to be afraid of letting Him run our lives? _____

_____

The only way not to be afraid is to live by faith. By faith we believe that He loves us and He will not bring us to harm. Read Jeremiah 29:11.

When we know that He will not harm us but only bring us good, we can live unafraid. When we live unafraid we listen for only His voice. We hear only His voice, and we keep in step with the Spirit. This process isn't us trying to do what Jesus would do. It is Jesus doing what He would do through us. This is obeying by faith.

4-TALK ABOUT OBEDIENCE

1. How aware are you when you get out of step with the Spirit?
2. Do you hear God's Spirit talking to you internally? What kind of things does the Spirit say to you?
3. When it comes to letting Him live through you, what are you afraid of?
4. Do you believe it is possible for you to be internally aware of the Spirit living through you?

After he [Joseph] had considered these things, an angel of the Lord suddenly appeared to him in a dream, saying, "Joseph, son of David, don't be afraid to take Mary as your wife" (Matt. 1:20).

The angel said to him: "Do not be afraid, Zechariah, because your prayer has been heard. Your wife Elizabeth will bear you a son, and you will name him John" (Luke 1:13).

The angel said to them, "Do not be afraid, for you see, I announce to you good news of great joy that will be for all the people" (Luke 2:10).

There is no fear in love; instead, perfect love drives out fear, because fear involves punishment. So the one who fears has not reached perfection in love (1 John 4:18).

"I know the plans I have for you"—this is the LORD's declaration— "plans for your welfare, not for disaster, to give you a future and a hope" (Jer. 29:11).

✦ DAY 3: OUT OF STEP: HIS VOICE AND HIS WORD

To others, Stephanie seemed to be so in tune to God that it was like He ordered her steps. People often wondered how she apparently knew what God wanted her to do at all times. When I asked her what her secret was, she replied, "It is no secret. I know His voice, and I know His Word." Stephanie had learned that keeping in step with the Spirit was a matter of listening.

1-A FAITH PRACTICE

One of the real secrets to obeying by faith is becoming sensitive to when you are walking out of step. This is totally a faith practice; because using just your own human wisdom, you will not know when you are out of God's will. In this session we are going to look at two practical ways that we can learn when we are out of step. Both of these practices operate correctly only when we approach them by faith.

> By faith Abraham, when he was called, obeyed and went out to a place he was going to receive as an inheritance; he went out, not knowing where he was going (Heb. 11:8).

Read Hebrews 11:8. How did Abraham obey the call of God?
☐ **He tried hard to please God.**
☐ **By faith.**
☐ **He stopped wondering.**
☐ **He followed a plan.**

Abraham went out "not knowing where he was going." As you hear and obey God's Word and His voice, you must trust that He is leading you. This is especially true when He tells you that you are out of step with the Spirit.

2-KNOWING BY HIS VOICE

The main way we know we are out of step is by listening to the voice of God. Just as a soldier knows he is not in step when his feet don't match the voice of the drill sergeant, we can know if we are out of step as God speaks directly to us.

Throughout the Bible we find many people who heard the voice of God. Sometimes He spoke in a whisper, as was Elijah's experience in 1 Kings 19. Sometimes He spoke in a loud, audible voice, as with the crowd that heard the voice of God in John 12:28-29. Jesus understood what God said; the crowd heard God's voice as thunder. Each situation when someone heard the voice of God was a little different. So how do you know if it is God's voice you are hearing or maybe just your own conscience? There are three keys.

KEY ONE: CONTENT

The number one thing God wants from you is a relationship. That is why He made you—to have a relationship with Him. God speaks to you to begin or strengthen His relationship with you.

When the God spoke to Jesus in Mark 1:11, what did He say?

_____

_____

_____

_____

_____

When God speaks to you, He will likely speak a word to build your relationship with Him. If you hear a voice telling you to read the Bible, it is probably not your conscience, definitely not Satan, and most likely God.

KEY TWO: MISSION

God is working in the world in the way that will bring glory to Him. At times His mission involves us. At times He speaks to us about our part in His work.

Read 1 Samuel 3:4-11 in your Bible. Why did God speak to Samuel?
☐ **To get his advice**
☐ **To startle the boy**
☐ **To prepare him for mission**
☐ **To form a network**

If you hear a voice telling you to witness to someone, it is probably not your conscience, definitely not Satan, and most likely God. Witnessing to someone is the kind of thing God would tell you to do.

"Father, glorify Your name!" Then a voice came from heaven: "I have glorified it, and I will glorify it again!" The crowd standing there heard it and said it was thunder. Others said, "An angel has spoken to Him!" (John 12:28-29).

A voice came from heaven: "You are My beloved Son; In You I take delight!" (Mark 1:11).

KEY THREE: SPIRIT

Although content and mission are good ways to tell the voice of God, the ultimate way is by the Spirit. Remember, He lives in you.

Read John 10:1-6 in your Bible. After reading this, what can you say about sheep?
☐ **Sheep know the shepherd's voice.**
☐ **Sheep know nothing.**
☐ **Sheep get in trouble all the time.**
☐ **Sheep are a pain to train.**

What does this story have to do with us? Read John 10:14-16. Check all that apply.
☐ **We are His sheep.**
☐ **We are wolves.**
☐ **As sheep we will know His voice.**
☐ **It is good to have a flock of sheep.**

Do you see? As Christians, we now have the Spirit in us and thus we are able to know His voice. This voice is generally a silent, inner voice; but when He speaks to us, He lets us know that it is from God.

3-KNOWING BY HIS WORD

God tells us we are out of step by His voice; but He uses other ways, especially the Bible.

> The word of God is living and effective and sharper than any two-edged sword, penetrating as far as to divide soul, spirit, joints, and marrow; it is a judge of the ideas and thoughts of the heart (Heb. 4:12).

THE BIBLE IS LIVING
Read Hebrews 4:12. How is the Word of God described?
☐ **The greatest book of all**
☐ **Holy**
☐ **Living, effective, sharp**
☐ **Thick**

The Bible is living. It penetrates into all the areas of your life. If while you are reading the Bible you read a verse that says to "love your enemies" (like Luke 6:27) and suddenly you realize you are acting mean toward someone, guess what? That feeling is God's Word poking at your heart. Why? It is showing you that you are out of step. Then, by faith you are able to believe He is in you and to allow Him to live through you and start loving that person.

THE BIBLE IS A LIGHT

The Bible not only pierces us but also guides us. Read Psalm 119:105; then fill in the blanks.

"Your W_____ is a l_____ for my f_____ and a l_____ on my p_____."

Your word is a lamp for my feet and a light on my path (Ps. 119:105).

God knows that even as we live and obey by faith, we need a concrete basis for our faith. God's Word serves as that foundation. Even though we now have the mind of Christ, we still need to fill that mind with the right information—God's Word. Jesus Himself was a student of the Scriptures. We must never get away from studying the Word.

The Bible lights the path; it keeps us on the path; it tells us when we are off the path; and it guides us as to how to get back on the path, back in step. Again, this is not a matter of us "doing better." Getting back requires faith and cooperation on our part.

4-TALK ABOUT OBEDIENCE

1. What does it mean to you to listen to God's voice and His Word by faith?
2. How can you know when it is God's voice speaking to you?
3. How does God use His Word to speak to you?
4. How can knowing His voice and His Word keep you in step with the Spirit?

★ DAY 4: OUT OF STEP: PRAYER AND PEOPLE

 Shelley believed it was God's will for her to marry Sid. Sid was good looking and wealthy. He even went to church with her on Christmas Eve.

Shelley's Christian friends and even her parents thought she had lost her mind. Sid was not a strong Christian. He was arrogant, untrustworthy, and lazy. Still, who were they to try to tell Shelley that she was out of God's will?

So the marriage happened. Six years later Sid dumped Shelley and found another woman. As Shelley tried to put her life back together she kept hearing her friends say, "I knew it was wrong from the start." Shelley wondered why those friends had never told her this back then.

In order to obey by faith, you need to keep in step with the Spirit. One of the keys to keeping in step is to know at once when you are out of step. You can know when you are out of step by God's voice and His Word. You can also know when you are out of step by prayer, parents, and the body of Christ.

1-KNOWING BY PRAYER

The voice of God can come to us at any time. However, there are special times when we seek God in prayer. During these prayers God will often tell us we are out of step.

Be silent before the LORD and wait expectantly for Him; do not be agitated by one who prospers in his way, by the man who carries out evil plans (Ps. 37:7).

We generally think prayer is us talking to God. Prayer is actually us communicating with God, and there is a difference. Read Psalm 37:7; then fill in the blanks.

"Be s_____ before the Lord and wait e_____ for Him."

Why would God tell us to be silent before Him? _____

_____

_____

Read Habakkuk 2:20. What does this verse encourage?

☐ Hard work before God
☐ Silence before God
☐ Losing control before God
☐ A well-planned worship experience

> The LORD is in His holy temple; let everyone on earth be silent in His presence (Hab. 2:20).

When we listen for God we begin by saying something along the lines of "God speak to Your servant; I am listening," and then we remain in quiet prayer waiting for God to speak. Often during these times of prayer, God will tell us that we are out of step. Other times God may actually tell us that we are walking in faith and allowing Christ to live through us. He tells us this to affirm and encourage.

Is it any wonder that in Luke 11:1 we see that the only thing the disciples ever asked Jesus to teach them was to pray? They knew prayer was essential to staying in step.

> He [Jesus] was praying in a certain place, and when He finished, one of His disciples said to Him, "Lord, teach us to pray, just as John also taught his disciples" (Luke 11:1).

2-KNOWING BY PARENTS

If you are still under your parents' authority (you live at home or your parents support you financially), you need to turn to your parents for protection. Your parents were given to you to protect you from getting out of step with God.

How does Ephesians 6:1 tell us to respond to our parents?

We are to obey in t_____ L_____.

> Children, obey your parents in the Lord, because this is right (Eph. 6:1).

This means we obey our parents by faith. By faith we believe that our parents are being used by God to protect us from getting out of step. When your parents warn you about something in your life, realize this may be God's way of telling you that you are out of step. Your parents are not perfect and may not always be right, but don't ever dismiss what they say as unimportant.

In Hebrews 11:23 we see a great example of this. How did Moses' parents protect him? _____

> By faith Moses, after he was born, was hidden by his parents for three months, because they saw that the child was beautiful, and they didn't fear the king's edict (Heb. 11:23).

Notice that Moses' parents did this by faith. They totally obeyed God's plan by faith.

NOTE: Even if your parents are not Christians, they are still part of God's plan to keep you in step.

3-KNOWING BY THE BODY

Your brothers and sisters in Christ are also responsible to keep you in step. When God tries to get through to you using His voice, His Word, your prayers, and your parents, and you still don't get it, don't be surprised if he sends a fellow Christian to hold you accountable.

Read 2 Samuel 12:1-13 in your Bible. What was David's reaction to Nathan? Check all that apply.
- ☐ **David hated Nathan.**
- ☐ **David realized Nathan was from God.**
- ☐ **David admitted he had sinned.**
- ☐ **David laughed at Nathan's story.**

No doubt about it, David was out of step with the Spirit. It would have been easy for David as the king to dismiss Nathan or even have him killed. But David realized that Nathan was sent from God to get him back in step.

God, create a clean heart for me and renew a steadfast spirit within me (Ps. 51:10).

After Nathan spoke to David, David did get back in step. His heart's desire is found in Psalm 51:10, where he prayed ...

"R_____ a s_____ spirit within me."

What David sought was for God's Spirit to control his spirit. He was looking to be souled out.

What should be your reaction when someone comes to you to show you where you are out of step?

O_____ by f_____.

4–TALK ABOUT OBEDIENCE

1. Why do we have a hard time listening to God in prayer?
2. Why do we have a hard time listening to our parents?
3. How has God used people in the body of Christ (your church) to call your attention to your being out of step?
4. How willing are you to know when you are out of step with God's Spirit?

DAY 5: BEYOND COMMITMENTS

Zach was moved by the youth camp speaker. When the invitation was given, he went forward to make his commitment. He promised to read the Bible daily, obey his parents, stop smoking, and refrain from sexual relationships with his girlfriend. When Zach got home from camp he felt really good for about three days. Then he broke all of his commitments in one day. What went wrong? The other youth just thought he wasn't sincere in his commitment. But the real problem was that although Zach knew his sin, he just didn't know how to obey by faith.

1–WHAT IS WRONG WITH COMMITMENTS?

The way most churches work is by relying on well-meaning people making commitments to God—commitments such as tithing and teaching Sunday School. Many youth ministries work the same way! Youth are taken off to camp, pumped up, and then asked to make commitments or rededications. Commitments may be anything, such as a commitment to witness, to sexual purity, to join the church. What could possibly be wrong with this approach to youth ministry?

Read 1 Samuel 15:22. What does this verse tell us?
☐ **All sacrifices must be burnt.**
☐ **We are not allowed to sacrifice.**
☐ **To obey is better than sacrifice.**
☐ **God delights in delightful things.**

Then Samuel said: "Does the LORD take pleasure in burnt offerings and sacrifices as much as in obeying the LORD? Look: to obey is better than sacrifice, to pay attention is better than the fat of rams" (1 Sam. 15:22).

What does "to obey is better than sacrifice" mean? Sacrifices in the Old Testament were rituals performed to cover the sins of the people, to be acts of worship, or to be acts of thankfulness.

God says that He is more concerned with obedience than with sacrifice. It is not that sacrifice is wrong, but God is looking for something more—obedience.

What does Romans 14:23 say about faith?

> **"Everything that is not from f_____ is s_____."**

What does that mean? When you carry out any action outside of faith—no matter how good the action—you are doing it in your own power, in your flesh. Your flesh cannot produce anything pleasing to God no matter how good it might look to others.

Only a commitment (a sacrifice) made in faith is pleasing to God. But even then, God is more interested in obedience than your sacrifice.

2-SURRENDER

We have looked at surrender and how it is the key to letting Jesus live through us. Now let's look at practical aspects of surrender.

SURRENDERING MY RIGHTS

As a free person living in a free country, you have certain rights. You have the right to life, liberty, and the pursuit of happiness. This means you can make of yourself whatever you wish. These are your rights. No one can take them away from you. You don't have to surrender these rights to anyone—unless, that is, you desire Jesus to live through you.

How did Paul describe the surrender of his own rights in 2 Corinthians 5:15? _____

_____

_____

This passage contains the concept of "living for Jesus." To live for Him means that by faith I assign to Him all my personal rights. It isn't my life anymore; it is His life. I no longer have a right to my life or even

Whoever doubts stands condemned if he eats, because his eating is not from faith, and everything that is not from faith is sin (Rom. 14:23).

He [Jesus] died for all so that those who live should no longer live for themselves, but for the One who died for them and was raised (2 Cor. 5:15).

to happiness. This can only happen as I believe by faith He is in me and by faith allow Him to live through me.

How do you do this in a practical way? One way is to come before God and give to Him all your personal rights. Pray something like this: "Lord, this isn't my life anymore; it is Yours. By faith I allow You to take me wherever You wish and do with me whatever You desire. Live Your will through me."

SURRENDERING MY WANTS

What do you want to be when you grow up? Where do you want to go? What do you hope to accomplish? At some point in time we all begin our want list. Our families and teachers may even encourage us to make our list big. Then we spend most of our lives pursuing our dreams, our wants.

What did Paul say about his "want list" in Philippians 3:7?

"Everything that was a g_____ to me, I have considered to be a l_____."

Paul actually had a new want list much different from his original. What did Paul now want according to Philippians 3:10?
- [ ] **To know Christ**
- [ ] **To know Christ's power**
- [ ] **To know Christ's sufferings**
- [ ] **To become like Him in death**

Actually all of these things made up Paul's new want list. Paul's list was a list made by faith that Christ was living in and through him. By faith he surrendered his old wants. Then by faith he received a new list of wants that were not his own wants.

To surrender your wants, dreams, and desires, begin by making a list of all the things you have gotten and all the things you want. (This is what Paul was doing in Philippians 3.) Then as Philippians 3:8 says, consider these things a loss. One way to do that is to verbally say, "These things mean nothing to me."

Everything that was a gain to me, I have considered to be a loss because of Christ (Phil. 3:7).

My goal is to know Him and the power of His resurrection and fellowship of His sufferings, being conformed to His death (Phil. 3:10).

More than that, I also consider everything to be a loss in view of the surpassing value of knowing Christ Jesus my Lord (Phil. 3:8).

Come now, you who say, "Today or tomorrow we will travel to such and such a city and spend a year there and do business and make a profit." You don't even know what tomorrow will bring—what your life will be! For you are a bit of smoke that appears for a little while, then vanishes. Instead, you should say, "If the Lord wills, we will live and do this or that" (Jas. 4:13-15).

When they came to Mysia, they tried to go into Bithynia, but the Spirit of Jesus did not allow them (Acts 16:7).

After he [Paul] had seen the vision, we immediately made efforts to set out for Macedonia, concluding that God had called us to evangelize them (Acts 16:10).

3-NO AGENDA

When you were a child, you began the day pretty much with no agenda. You just did what your parents had planned for you to do. When they said eat, you ate; when they said sleep, you slept. Now you probably approach each day with an agenda. The problem with that is that it doesn't give God a chance to call the shots unless you consider God's agenda before making your own.

This is what James was saying in James 4:13-15. What do you think James would say about our agendas? _____
_____
_____
_____

Of all the people in the early church, no one was more "on task" than Paul. What was on Paul's agenda in Acts 16:7?
☐ Start a church in Rome
☐ Enter Bithynia
☐ Write a letter to Timothy
☐ Get out of jail

What prevented Paul from completing his agenda? _____
_____
_____
_____

Who gave Paul a new agenda in Acts 16:10? _____
_____

Having no agenda can mean you are totally controlled by Him. He orders your very steps. This is all possible because of the intimate fellowship you have with Him.

4-TALK ABOUT OBEDIENCE

1. Have you ever made a "commitment" in your own power? If so, what was it and how did it go?
2. Why is it hard for some people to surrender rights and wants?
3. What is on your agenda for the next few weeks of school?
4. Based on what you have learned this week, how does someone obey by faith?

A SOULED OUT YOU

For the past several weeks you have studied about being souled out. You have learned about how Christ lives inside of you. You now know that He wants to control your soul.

The problem is that the flesh (even Satan) also wants to control your soul. It is not that when the flesh is in control of your soul you will become an axe murderer; you just won't have the fruit of the Spirit (love, joy, peace, and so forth). And when the flesh is in control of your soul, you will not be what God desires you to be.

So how do you allow the Spirit of God to control you? By faith you turn your mind, emotions, and will over to Him. It is an ongoing, day-by-day, even moment-by-moment surrender to Him.

When you turn it over to Him, you are actually out of the way; and it is just Him in your soul. Your soul has become souled out.

You don't do any of this by trying harder or even studying more. You do this all by faith. Faith asks the Holy Spirit to control the mind, emotions, and will; and then faith believes He is actually in control.

This book has explained in human words a very spiritual process. Yet if you have faithfully studied this book, we believe by faith that the Spirit has taught you these spiritual truths. Now all that is necessary for you to be souled out is your own willingness to let Him take control.

This is our prayer that you will allow Him to control your mind, your emotions, and your will. In fact we pray you will begin to see that it is His mind, His emotions, and His will.

1. *Blue Letter Bible.* "Dictionary and Word Search for 'stoicheo (Strong's 4748)'". Blue Letter Bible. 1996-2002. 4 Mar 2004. <*http://www.blueletterbible.org/cgi-bin/words.pl?word=4748&page=1*>.

GUIDELINES FOR LEADING GROUP SESSIONS

If you are leading students through *Souled Out*, the following material will give you general instructions for leading your group. There are two basic approaches to studying *Souled Out*—a six-session approach and a fifteen-session approach.

THE SIX-SESSION APPROACH
1. The study is completed in six weeks.
2. Students read all five sections of material in each chapter before the session.
3. Students memorize the weekly Bible verse and do the daily devotional readings.
4. Group session is largely discussion.

THE FIFTEEN-SESSION APPROACH
1. The study is completed in fifteen (50-minute) sessions which can be once a week or at different intervals. Two days of material is studied per session.
2. All work is done in the group sessions. Leaders may occasionally need to prepare simple learning aids before the session.
3. Group sessions are largely discussion, but each session contains some interactive learning activities.
4. The group leader guides students through the study as the group reads together all material and answers all response questions.
5. This approach can be done in any weekday setting or even on Sunday morning.

In preparation for each session, work through the chapter yourself. This will help you answer any questions the students might have about the questions in the chapters. The fill-in-the-blank activities are straight from Scripture, which is printed in the margins unless the passage is too long to print.

THE SIX-SESSION APPROACH

SESSION 1
THE NATURE OF PEACE

○ Say, **This six-week study deals with the body, soul, and spirit and how these interact.** Mention that there are more than 130 verses in the Bible that talk about the body (flesh), about an equal number that talk about the soul, and an even greater number that talk about the Spirit.

○ Call attention to diagram 1 on page 10. Draw the diagram on chart paper, showing the relationship between body, soul, and spirit. Point to the spirit "circle" and explain, **God's Spirit is present with your spirit.** Explain that the middle circle represents the soul—the mind, the emotions, and the will.

○ Explain that we are going to be looking at how God's Spirit can gain control of our entire life—body, soul, and spirit. There are three key parts of us that need to be controlled in order for our souls to be "souled out" to God: our minds, our emotions, and our wills.

○ Ask, **Why is the mind so important in determining who you are and who you become?** Ask a student to read aloud Proverbs 23:7 as you discuss this answer.

○ Next, divide the group into pairs and instruct each pair to come up with a definition of peace. After a few minutes allow each pair to share their answer. Read the section "Biblical Peace" (3.1)* Explain that peace is both outward unity and inward harmony.

○ Ask, **Which is more difficult for you—having unity without or harmony within?**

○ Ask: **We know peace comes from Jesus, but why does it come from Him? What did He do that brings us peace?** Emphasize that Jesus doesn't just bring peace; He is peace!

○ Call upon a student to explain how Jesus is complete inwardly and unified outwardly.

○ Read "Pursuing Peace of Mind" (5.1). Carefully review the four parts of the definition, asking if anyone has questions about any parts of the definition of *peace*.

○ Write these three words on a chalkboard or tear sheet: *surrender, renewal, warfare.* Explain that these are the keys to allowing your mind to be controlled by the Spirit that is already within.

○ Ask, **Who can explain what it means to surrender?**

○ Lead the group to say the memory verse for the week, 2 Thessalonians 3:16, together.

○ Review the devotional readings for the week.

○ Conclude the session by asking if there were any response questions that anyone was unsure of. Close the session by praying together this week's "Prayer Thought": "Father, control my mind and bring me Your peace. Your peace, Lord, Your peace."

*(3.1) stands for Day 3, Section 1 – All references to the student material will be shortened in this way. The first number refers to the day, and the second number refers to the section.

SESSION 2
FROM THE RUT TO REST

○ Start the session with a brief prayer asking God to teach this material to His children.

○ Begin by asking if anyone has ever known anyone like Moody Judy.

○ Ask, **What is the confession trap, and why do we get caught in this trap?** (Answer: We confess, but we fail to take steps necessary to be controlled by Christ.) Ask for volunteers to share about their own struggles with the confession trap. Ask, **Has anything made a difference or are you still in this rut?**

○ Divide the group into two teams. Assign one team "Renewal" (1.2) and the other team "Warfare" (1.3). Instruct the teams to prepare to share their understanding of these steps in having the mind controlled by Christ. Then lead a discussion on the importance of each.

○ Call upon a student to read Psalm 133. Ask a volunteer to explain this Psalm to the group.

○ Ask, **What are the three principles on which peace among brothers is achieved?** (Answer: community, purpose, and salt) Call upon youth to explain each principle.

○ As a way of review say, **Outward unity and peace comes when everyone (principle 1) works for a common goal (principle 2) that is accomplished by Christ in us (principle 3).**

○ Ask, **How can our emotions take away our peace of mind?**

○ Ask: **What are the keys to staying "cool in the furnace"? What does it mean to you to have your emotions overridden by faith?**

○ Ask: **Why is our gospel a gospel of peace? How are you an ambassador of peace?**

○ Explain that in the Bible, rest is a central, yet seldom explained concept that was highlighted when on the seventh day God "rested" from all His work.

○ Ask for students to define the concept of rest as they have studied the concept thus far.

○ Read "Rest from Weariness" (5.2). Emphasize the process of (1) Taking His yoke, (2) Learning from Him, (3) Finding rest.

○ Review this week's memory verse, Matthew 11:28, by leading students to say this verse together.

○ Review Ephesians 4–6, which the students read in their devotional time this week. Review the answers to any response questions that were a problem this week.

SESSION 3
GOD'S OFFER OF JOY

○ Begin by reviewing the memory verse for this week, John 15:11, and then asking the group to briefly share about their devotional reading in John 15–17 the past week. Review any questions that were a problem.

○ Ask, **What are the constant themes that run through this passage?** (Answer: He lives in us, and we live in Him.)

○ Ask: **What is it about you that distinguishes you from animals?** (Answer: the spirit) **What is it about you that distinguishes you from other people?** (Answer: the soul)

○ Divide the group into two teams. Instruct one team to think of all the emotions that are produced by the "Spirit" and the other team to think of all the emotions that are produced by the "flesh."
  After teams report, ask, **On a regular basis how aware are you of who or what—Spirit or flesh—is controlling your emotions?**

○ Read aloud the story of Susan under "What Is Joy and Where Does It Come From?" (2.0) Ask: **Does anyone know someone like Susan who is trying to find joy in all sorts of places? Why do some people who grew up going to church just assume the answer to what they are looking for is not found in Jesus?**

○ Ask, **How would you define real joy?** (Answer: Joy comes when we see and experience the glory of God.)

○ Review the ways that real joy will change us: (1) It changes our strength. (2) It changes our appearance. (3) It changes our purpose.

○ Ask: **Why will "trying" hard to find joy not bring someone much joy? What are the ways you have tried to make yourself happy? What were the results?**

○ Read John 10:10. Explain that Jesus desires to give us an abundant life with true joy. It is not so much that we have to find anything, but rather we just receive what He is already in the process of giving us.

○ Ask: **How can a failure on your part to accept God's offer of joy cause a loss of joy? What do you need to do to accept His offer?**

○ Say, **There are two things that actually happen in our good times that can cause us to lose joy—unrealistic expectations and the natural letdown.** Call upon students to explain both.

○ Ask, **What is the key to having joy in the midst of good times?** (Answer: Give the glory to God.)

○ Conclude by praying this week's "Prayer Thought" together as a group: "Let me see Your glory, Lord, Your glory."

SESSION 4
JOY DAY TO DAY

◯ Lead the entire group in saying the memory verses for this week, 1 Thessalonians 5:16-18. Call upon several in the group to share any insights they gained from this week's devotional readings in Psalms. Review any questions that were a problem this week.

◯ Review this week's "Prayer Thought": "Father, cause me to focus on You. To see You, oh God, and not my circumstances." Ask how many have prayed that prayer this past week.

◯ Ask, **Why do most people not understand the reason and nature of true celebration?** (Answer: They focus on themselves and not God.)

◯ Ask, **Why does the real celebration never end?** (Answer: It is about God.)

◯ Ask students to form two groups. Instruct groups to prepare a brief oral presentation entitled "How Bad Times Can Lead to Joy." After a few minutes, allow groups to share their presentations.

◯ Emphasize to the group that bad times can bring joy because they are used by God for His glory and they can bring good results. Ask youth to share examples from their own lives of these two concepts.

◯ Read to the group "Joy All the Time?" (3.1) Ask, **Do you really think it is possible to have joy all the time?**

◯ Call upon a student to read 2 John 4. Ask, **How many of you feel that your greatest joy is seeing others walking in the truth?**

◯ Read Hebrews 10:24-25 and discuss the importance of fellowship in the body as it relates to joy.

◯ Read the story of Steve (4.0). Ask, **How many of you have felt like Steve when it comes to giving?**

◯ Remind students of the three main motivations for giving: (1) Obedience, (2) It Changes Our Focus, (3) It Changes Others. Ask, **Which of these three motivates you to give?**

◯ Ask students to share about where they are in their personal giving. Do they tithe? Do they give regularly? Do they not give? Emphasize that God wants us to give because it actually brings us joy. Share your own experience of how giving brings joy.

◯ Ask: **Why does the world need joy at this time? What can we give them that will also give them joy?**

◯ Remind students that when people hear about Jesus, they have the chance for joy.

◯ Remind the youth that they cannot bring anyone to Jesus or give anyone any joy. It all must be done by God.

◯ Close by asking a student to read aloud John 6:44.

SESSION FIVE
OBEYING BY FAITH

○ Read aloud Hebrews 11. Ask, **What did all these people have in common?** (Answer: They obeyed God by faith.)

○ Call upon a student to read aloud "What Is the Will?" (1.1). Emphasize that our wills lead directly to our actions. We do what we will to do.

○ Ask, **What is God's desire for your will?** (Answer: Replace it with His own)

○ Divide the group into three teams. Assign each team a different "problem" of the human will (2.1, 2.2, 2.3). Each team is to explain the problem in a brief presentation to the group.

○ Read John 6:63. Ask, **Why can't the Spirit and the flesh work together to guide the will into right actions?**

○ Read the story of Andrew (3.0). Ask, **Can anyone relate to this kind of behavior?**

○ Read James 1:13-15 and Romans 1:32. Ask: **What would you say to a person who says he sinned because God led him into sin? What would you say to a person who says she sinned because the devil made her do it?**

○ Ask, **Why won't just trying harder make a difference in our sinful habits?** (Answer: Trying harder is flesh trying to control flesh ... it won't work.)

○ Say: **The material this week was trying to convince you that you in your natural state are a worse sinner than a drug dealer or** runaway father. **Did you think that must have been a misprint?** Read 1 Timothy 1:15 aloud. Say, **Do you think that verse must be a misprint as well?**

○ Ask, **Since these are not misprints, why are we and Paul lumped into the group of the "worst sinners on earth"?**

○ Ask, **What does seeing yourself as a horrible sinner have to do with obeying by faith?**

○ Ask, **What is the real battle for the will?**

○ Read "A Tale of Two Trees" (4.3). Explain how Jesus reversed the decision made by Adam.

○ Call for volunteers to explain the two main parts of obeying by faith: "Believing Christ Is in You" (5.2) and "Allowing Him to Live Out Obedience to His Father Through You" (5.3).

○ Review the memory verse for the week, Colossians 2:6, by reciting it together as a group.

○ Ask if anyone had questions about the answers to any of the questions this week.

○ Close by praying together the "Prayer Thought": "Lord, take control of my will and live through me. Live through me."

SESSION SIX
KEEPING IN STEP

○ Begin by saying together this week's memory verse, Galatians 5:25. Review the devotional readings; then answer any questions students found difficult answering this week.

○ Divide the group into two teams. Instruct one team to give a verbal report explaining the "First Exchange" (1.1) and the second team to report on the "Second Exchange" (1.2).

○ Call upon a student to read Galatians 2:20. Say, **The great exchange is essential to obeying because only when Jesus is living in me can I really obey the Father.**

○ Review the process of "Surrender, Renewal, Warfare" (1.3). Share a testimony of how this has worked in your life. Allow students to share how they have been able to apply "Surrender, Renewal, Warfare" to walk in consistent obedience.

○ Read "How to Keep in Step" (2.1). Explain that keeping in step is possible when we become internally aware of the Spirit's voice.

○ Say: **In order to keep in step, we have to hear the Spirit's voice. Yet if we are afraid of what God might say, we will not hear His voice.** Ask, **What is the answer to living unafraid?** (2.3) (Answer: By faith believing God has good, not harm, planned for us.)

○ Ask, **What are the keys to knowing it is God's voice you are hearing?** (3.2) (Answer: Content, Mission, and Spirit)

○ Briefly review how Content, Mission, and Spirit (3.2) let us know if we are really hearing God's voice or some other voice, like the voice of Satan or the voice of our own flesh.

○ Ask, **How does God's Word let us know we are out of step?** (4.0)

○ Encourage students to continue in God's Word after this study ends. Review what they will read for their individual devotional times.

○ Ask, **When you pray, do you make a special effort to listen for God to speak?** Share how you listen for God to speak. (4.1)

○ Ask a student to read "Knowing by Parents" (4.2). Ask, **How are your parents here to keep you in step with the Spirit?**

○ Ask, **What roll do Christian friends play in keeping us in step with the Spirit?** (4.3)

○ Ask, **What is wrong with making commitments?** (5.1) (Answer: Nothing, if they are made by faith; but most are made by human will, which equals the flesh.)

○ Explain why God wants us to surrender our rights and wants. (5.2)

○ Say: **Obeying by faith means we must be open to the Spirit's leading at all times. At times God may desire for you to do something that was not on your schedule for that day.** Ask, **How does that make you feel?**

○ Conclude with a circular prayer. Direct each person in turn to pray the same short prayer, "Jesus, take my will and let it be only Your will. Only Your will, Jesus."

THE FIFTEEN-SESSION APPROACH

SESSION 1

STUDY: CHAPTER 1, DAYS 1 AND 2

Getting Started: 5 minutes
Direct students to read the story of Katie at the beginning of Day 1. Lead them to discuss what they think Katie's problem was.

The Study: 40 minutes
1.1: Read this section and complete the answers as a group. Encourage youth to share if they have asked Jesus to come into their hearts.

1.2 and 1.3: Divide the group into two teams. Assign one team to read and complete Section 2 and the other team to complete Section 3. Assign the teams to a debate—one team arguing that the body is more powerful than the soul and the other arguing that the soul is more powerful than the body.

After the debate explain that the soul without the power of the Spirit is no match for the flesh (body), and that is why people sin and cannot stop. Before moving on, review the answers the students recorded in the response spaces.

2.1: Call on volunteers to read the introduction to Day 2 as well as Section 1. Work together as a group to complete the response activities. Ask students to share how their mind shapes who they are. Share examples from your own life.

2.2: Before reading this section ask students to record on a sheet of paper the random thoughts they have had today. Then read the section and complete the response activities as a group. Briefly discuss the sources of what appear to be random thoughts.

2.3: Read Section 3 and complete the response activities as a group. Explain that God left us with a free mind able to focus on whatever it will in order for us to live by faith.

Wrap Up: 5 minutes
Discuss as a group the questions in "Talk About Peace" from both Days 1 and 2. Conclude by praying the "Prayer Thought" from the chapter introduction.

SESSION 2

STUDY: CHAPTER 1, DAYS 3 AND 4

Getting Started: 5 minutes
Read the introduction to Day 3. Ask students to discuss in small groups and then write in their books a paragraph entitled "What Is Peace?"

The Study: 40 minutes
3.1: Read this section to the youth and complete the response activities as a group.

Write *shalom* and *eirene* on tear sheets and direct youth to come up with the one English word they feel best defines each word. Note: Several words would be correct answers, but focus on "completeness" or "soundness" for *shalom* and "unity" or "harmony" for *eirene*.

3.2: Ask a volunteer to read this section as students complete the response activities. Assign students to groups of three. Give each group paper and instruct them to create a drawing of the "Price of Peace."

3.3: Instruct students to read this section on

their own and answer the questions. Then review the correct answers.

4.1: Read the introduction and the beginning of this section down to the "Jesus Is Complete—Inwardly" heading. Then divide the group into two teams. Assign one team to study "Jesus Is Complete—Inwardly" and the other team to study "Jesus Is Unified—Outwardly." Give the teams a few minutes; then call for the teams to present what they have studied. Review all the response material.

4.2: Study together Section 2, answering all the questions as a group. Go around your group and ask each person to finish the statement, **I used to look for peace in** _____.

4.3: Ask a student to read Section 3. Explain that the pursuit of peace begins inside. Pray for the Spirit to produce peace in each person.

Wrap Up: 5 minutes
Review the memory verse, 2 Thessalonians 3:16, saying it together a few times and then calling upon individuals to say the verse.

SESSION 3

STUDY: CHAPTER 1, DAY 5; CHAPTER 2, DAY 1

Getting Started: 5 minutes
Call upon someone to read the story about Moody Judy in the introduction to Day 1, Chapter 2. Ask if anyone has ever known someone like this or has ever been like this.

The Study: 40 minutes
5.1: Read the first two paragraphs of Section 1 and then write the definition of inner peace on a tear sheet.

Assign students to one of four teams to report on the four portions of the definition of peace. Direct each team to look up the Scripture for their part of the definition and prepare to read it and report the answers to the group. Ask each team to read their portion of the definition, the Scripture passage, and the answers.

5.2: Read Section 2 to the group, leading students to complete the multiple choice question as a group. Then ask students to form two teams. Assign each team to come up with a brief skit showing what it means to "surrender." After sufficient time, allow teams to present the skits.

1.1: Read this section to the group, completing the response activities as you go. Ask: **How is "confession" related to the step of "surrender"?** (Answer: They are the same concept.) Ask: **How does confession become a trap?** (Answer: Without the next two steps it becomes a vicious cycle.)

1.2: Read Section 2 to the group, completing the response activities as you go. Ask for a volunteer to define renewal.

1.3: Call upon a student to read Section 3. Share your own personal experiences of spiritual warfare. If possible, invite another adult or older youth to come to your group and share his or her experience with spiritual warfare.

Wrap Up: 5 minutes
At the end of 1.2 and 1.3 are two short prayers—one for Renewal and one for Warfare. Assign two students to pray each of these prayers as you close.

SESSION 4

STUDY: CHAPTER 2, DAYS 2 AND 3

Getting Started: 5 minutes
Begin by saying, **Today we are going to look at the foundation for peace among Christian brothers and sisters (Day 2) and also how to have peace in fearful situations (Day 3).** Ask students to think about a time when they did not have peace among brothers or peace in a fearful situation. Ask: **What effect did this lack of peace have on your life? Do you think it is possible to have peace in these areas?**

The Study: 40 minutes
2.1: Read Psalm 133 aloud from your Bible. Ask, **What do you think this Psalm has to do with each of you getting along with the others?**

Read the story about Sean and Kenn in the introduction to Day 2 and then call for volunteers to read Section 1 and complete the response activities.

2.2: Read Section 2 to the group, leading students to complete the responses as you read.

Divide the group into two teams and instruct each team to discuss the unity that presently exists in the youth group. Ask teams to share their discussions.

2.3: Form groups of two and assign each group to study a different principle of outer peace. Ask the various pairs to make a report on their assigned principle. Quickly review all the response questions before moving on.

3.1: Read the introductory story and Section 1 to the group. Ask students to respond to the questions as you read. Ask for them to share situations where circumstances, not faith, brought fear and not peace.

3.2: Assign students to read Section 2 on their own while you write the three factors that gave the young men peace on a chalkboard or a tear sheet. Review these three factors, explaining and then giving examples from your own life.

3.3: Ask, **How can our emotions be overridden by faith?** (Answer: By surrender and removal of our emotions.)

Read Section 3 to the group. Say, **When by faith we find our emotions are removed from us—they are now under His control—we will find we have no fear of any situation, even the toughest situation.** Ask, **Do you think it is possible to see this happen in your life?**

Lead students in praying the prayers in the "Surrender" subsection and the "Removal" subsection.

Wrap Up: 5 minutes
Lead youth to pray the "Prayer Thought" from the introduction of Chapter 2.

SESSION 5

STUDY: CHAPTER 2, DAYS 4 AND 5

Getting Started: 5 minutes
Read the story about Todd in the introduction to Day 4. Ask students if they have ever known anyone like Todd. Ask, **Is allowing Jesus to live through you in this way something you want to see happen?**

The Study: 40 minutes
4.1: Direct students to work in teams to read and complete Section 1 and then either write a poem or draw a picture showing that we are no longer God's enemies. Review the answers.

4.2: Read Section 2 and answer the questions as a group. Ask, **How is sharing the gospel actually about sharing peace?**

4.3: Form small teams and instruct each team to study Section 3 and then develop a short skit that shows our job as ambassadors. Call on teams to perform their skits.

5.1: Read the story of J.D. and Section 1 to the group, completing the activities as you read. Ask, **How would you define rest?**

5.2: Form pairs and assign each pair one of the three steps to resting from weariness. Direct pairs to share about their step. Then review the practical applications for rest from weariness.

5.3: Read this section to the group. Review responses to the questions. Share from your life what it means to enter this rest.

Wrap Up: 5 minutes
Review the memory verse for Chapter 2, Matthew 11:28. Remind students that the key to having inner peace is allowing their minds to be controlled by the Spirit so that they see, understand, and believe that they are already complete in Christ.

SESSION 6

STUDY: CHAPTER 3, DAYS 1 AND 2

Getting Started: 5 minutes
On note cards write down situations that bring joy and other emotions. (*Examples: You get a new car for your birthday. You fail algebra.*) Give each student a card. Ask students to read their cards and tell what emotion they would have in that situation. Say, **Today we start a study that will teach us how to have joy that is not based on circumstances and situations.**

The Study: 40 minutes
1.1: Read Section 1 to the group and lead them to complete the response activities. Ask students if they are aware that Christ is in them. Ask if they are aware that He is in control of them.

1.2 and 1.3: Divide the group into two teams. Instruct one team to study Section 2 and the other team to study Section 3. Direct each team to make a report by reading the material in their section, including answers, as they explain "Why We Have Emotions" and "Getting in Touch with Your Emotions."

2.0 and 2.1: Read the story about Susan in the introduction to Day 2. Ask if anyone can relate to Susan's experience.

Instruct students to read together Section 1 and complete the response questions. Ask, **Why do you think real joy is primarily an inward thing?**

2.2: Read Section 2 to the group, leading students to complete each response question. Ask: **Why is searching for joy not a bad thing? What would you say to your friends seeking joy in the things of this world?**

2.3: Divide the group into teams again and tell each team to complete Section 3. Then instruct teams to create a drawing (on a poster or a tear sheet) depicting joy as seeing God's glory.

Wrap Up: 5 minutes
Review the "Prayer Thought" for Chapter 3. Pray this as a group, directing each person to say the same simple prayer.

SESSION 7

STUDY: CHAPTER 3, DAYS 3 AND 4

Getting Started: 5 minutes

Before the session write *joy* on a note card, place it in a small box, and wrap the box in gift wrap. As you begin, ask students, **Who wants a gift?** Choose one student and give him or her the box. Watch what happens next. Does the student open the box? Of course. Explain to the group that a gift doesn't really become yours until you accept it. Say, **Today we are going to learn about accepting God's offer of joy.**

The Study: 40 minutes

3.1: Divide the group into three teams and assign each team to study and report on one of the three ways joy changes someone. Allow each team to present a report, explaining how joy changes our strength, our appearance, and our purpose. Review all response questions in Section 1.

3.2 and 3.3: Ask students to form two teams. Assign one team Section 2 and the other team Section 3.

Organize a debate with the first team arguing, "You can find joy if you look hard enough," and the second team arguing, "You can't find joy by looking hard; joy must find you."

After the debate, review the material from Sections 2 and 3, covering all the responses to questions.

4.1: Read Section 1 to the group, leading students to respond to the questions. Ask, **Why do many people reject God's offer of joy?**

4.2: Instruct students to study Section 2 on their own. When they have finished, review their responses. Discuss the importance of responding to God's offer of joy while still young.

4.3: Read Section 3 to the group. Lead students in praying both of the short prayers in this section.

Wrap Up: 5 minutes

Lead students to read together the memory verse, John 15:11. Lead them to repeat the verse as a group a few times. Then call upon individuals to say the verse from memory.

SESSION 8

STUDY: CHAPTER 3, DAY 5; CHAPTER 4, DAY 1

Getting Started: 5 minutes

Read Kelly's story in the introduction to Day 5 and Anna and Demico's story from Day 1. Ask, **What common mistakes are found in all three of these lives?** (Answers: Trying to find joy in things, failure to understand God's ways, no idea about seeing God's glory.)

The Study: 40 minutes

5.1: Read Section 1 and lead students to answer the response questions. Ask: **Can anyone remember a time when you should have had joy, but you did not? What happened?**

5.2: Give each student a sheet of paper. Assign everyone to read Section 2 on their own and answer the questions. Direct students to write a paragraph about "Why Good Times Can Bring Big Sorrow." Collect these unsigned and read some to the group. Before moving on, review the material and the questions.

5.3: Read Section 3 as students provide answers to the questions. Ask, **What is the key to having joy in good times?** *(Answer: Giving the glory to God.)*

1.1: Call for volunteers to read Section 1 as you work as a group to complete the response activities. Then give each student a note card to write down how they would celebrate receiving a brand-new car. Ask volunteers to share their responses.

1.2: Read Section 2 to the group, answering the response questions together. Ask, **What is the key to letting the good times roll?**

1.3: Divide the group into two teams. Instruct each team to read and complete Section 3. Direct youth to create a drawing on poster board or tear sheet depicting the party never ending for the Christian.

Wrap Up: 5 minutes

Enlist a guest to come to your group time and share how he or she gave the glory to God in the midst of incredibly good times. Ask the guest to lead your group in a closing prayer.

SESSION 9

STUDY: CHAPTER 4, DAYS 2 AND 3

Getting Started: 5 minutes

Bring a copy of a recent newspaper to the session. Instruct students to search through the paper to find examples of tragic accidents and situations. Ask, **Is it possible for people facing these kinds of situations to have any joy in their lives?**

The Study: 40 minutes

2.1: Read Section 1 to the group, leading them to answer the response questions as you go. Ask, **Why is it not productive to long for the "good old days" when bad times happen?**

2.2: Divide the group into two teams. Ask one team to read "First: Bad Times for Good Results" and the other team to read "Second: Bad Times Can Bring Glory to God." Lead students to complete the questions as they read.

Direct each team to create a skit that explains or demonstrates their assignment. Ask groups to present their skits then review all the material in their assigned section.

2.3: Read Section 3 to the group, answering the questions as you read. Review the two meanings of sowing: dying and giving. Ask, **How does sowing, dying, and giving lead to joy?**

3.1: Direct youth to read and complete Section 1 on their own. Review the material and the answers. Ask, **What is the key to joy all the time?** *(Answer: Christ controlling a person.)*

3.2 and 3.3: Allow students to choose a partner. Give each pair a sheet of paper. Assign each pair to read either Section 2 or 3 and then write a paragraph summary of the assigned section.

Ask the pairs to read their paragraphs. Review the material in Sections 2 and 3, including answers to the response questions.

Wrap Up: 5 minutes

As a group, review the memory verses for the week, 1 Thessalonians 5:16-18. Ask each student to repeat the passage to the person next to him, going around the group so that each person says it once and hears it once. Close in prayer.

SESSION 10
STUDY: CHAPTER 4, DAYS 4 AND 5

Getting Started: 5 minutes
Give each student a blank note card. Ask students to write down how much money they have given to the church in the past month. Collect these unsigned cards. Then give the students another blank card. Ask them to write down how much money they have earned, been given, or received for allowance during the past month. Collect these unsigned cards. Compare the amounts. Say: **Today we are going to talk about giving both money and our faith, and how we can give these by faith and find joy in the process.**

The Study: 40 minutes
4.1: Read the story about Steve as well as Section 1 to the group, leading students to complete the response activities as you go. Ask, **Why are we to give?** (Answer: God says to give.) Ask, **How does giving bring us joy?** (Answer: When we obey God by faith, God gets glory. When He gets glory, we see His glory and we experience joy.)

4.2 and 4.3: Ask students to form two teams. Assign one team Section 2 and the other team Section 3. Direct teams to read their sections and complete the response activities.

Instruct the teams to create a picture or a poem that expresses how giving changes our focus and how it changes other people. Direct groups to present their work and then review the material and the response questions.

5.1: Read the story about Ahmad to the group. Ask, **How does knowing that billions of people in our world have no joy make you feel?**

Read Section 1 to the group and answer the questions. Ask, **Why do so many people try to find joy through sin?**

5.2: Assign students to read Section 2 on their own; then review the material. Ask, **Why will just trying to cheer people up not work?**

5.3: Read Section 3 to the group, answering the questions as you go. Ask, **What is necessary for true conversion?** (Answer: Christ doing the work through us.) Ask, **Why does conversion of someone else always bring us joy?** (Answer: It is the work of God, and as such we see His glory and we get joy.)

Wrap Up: 5 minutes
Review the "Prayer Thought" for Week 4. Pray this prayer together as a closing prayer.

SESSION 11
STUDY: CHAPTER 5, DAYS 1 AND 2

Getting Started: 5 minutes
Bring candy bars for everyone in your group. Give each person a candy bar, but then tell students that they will have to wait until next week to eat it. Ask, **Who thinks they can take this candy bar home and have the willpower to not eat it for one week?** Read the story of Candace and talk about the problem of willpower.

The Study: 40 minutes
1.1: Read Section 1 to the group, leading students to complete the questions as you read. Ask, **How does will lead directly to actions?** Share a personal experience of your will going directly against your mind or emotions into action.